Eternal Submission

Eternal Submission

A Biblical and Theological Examination

JONATHAN J. ROUTLEY

WIPF & STOCK · Eugene, Oregon

ETERNAL SUBMISSION
A Biblical and Theological Examination

Copyright © 2019 Jonathan J. Routley. All rights reserved. Except for brief quotations in critical publications or reviews, no part of this book may be reproduced in any manner without prior written permission from the publisher. Write: Permissions, Wipf and Stock Publishers, 199 W. 8th Ave., Suite 3, Eugene, OR 97401.

Wipf & Stock
An Imprint of Wipf and Stock Publishers
199 W. 8th Ave., Suite 3
Eugene, OR 97401

www.wipfandstock.com

PAPERBACK ISBN: 978-1-5326-7328-3
HARDCOVER ISBN: 978-1-5326-7329-0
EBOOK ISBN: 978-1-5326-7330-6

Manufactured in the U.S.A.   APRIL 17, 2019

To Janelle, whose life of love, joy,
and sacrifice displays Christ daily to all.

Contents

Preface | ix
Acknowledgements | xv

Chapter 1 The Question of Eternal Submission | 1
Chapter 2 The Opposition to Eternal Submission | 16
Chapter 3 A Biblical Examination of Eternal Submission | 30
Chapter 4 The Witness of the Church and Eternal Submission | 62
Chapter 5 A Theological Examination of Eternal Submission | 79
Chapter 6 The Implications of Eternal Submission | 122

Bibliography | 131
Index | 139

Preface

I BEGAN THIS JOURNEY years ago while a graduate student at Faith Baptist Theological Seminary in Ankeny, Iowa. My professor at that time, Dr. Myron Houghton, taught a class called advanced theology proper. This was my first in-depth exposure to Trinitarian theology and it was captivating. Among other texts, we read Letham's *The Holy Trinity*, and I soaked in every word. My professor went out of his way to guard against what I have come to view as a Western overemphasis on God's oneness without the necessary Eastern balancing focus on his threeness. He even suggested that in explaining the Trinity we start with the three divine persons and then proceed to the one shared divine nature. I am immensely grateful for that very formative class.

After graduating from Faith with a master of arts in theological studies, I went on to study at Western Seminary in Portland, Oregon. Upon entering the master of theology program, my first seminar was on the Trinity, taught by J. Ryan Lister. This was the spring of 2016. My affection for Trinitarian studies was renewed, and during that one-week intensive course our small class thought deeply about the mystery of the triune God. I wrote two papers in that class that would help to guide my later studies. One was a book review of Kevin Giles' *Jesus and the Father*. The other was a paper arguing for the eternal submission of the Son, which became much of the basis for this present work. I greatly enjoyed the research and reading for that paper. I had little idea of the coming blog war that would take place later that summer.

Preface

The summer came, and with it the beginning of the great Trinity debate of 2016. I read and observed much over the summer, and when the time came in the fall to choose a topic for a ThM thesis, I knew what I wanted to write about. A great deal of what was being argued about in the summer of 2016 had already been worked through in article conversations between Kevin Giles and Robert Letham, among others, years earlier. There were some newer emphases (which I attempt to discuss in this book), but even many of these were reworkings of older arguments.

In researching this important theological issue, a number of things became clear. First, this is as much an issue of authority as is any other biblical debate. So much of the conversation surrounding eternal submission depends on one's answer to the question of authority. Where does authority ultimately lie for the believer? Historically, evangelicals would immediately sound forth the battle cry for Scripture, and rightly so. But are there any other sources of authority? And if so, how authoritative are those authorities? Can we look to the history of the church as an authoritative guide? It seems clear that some view church history, and particularly "Nicene Trinitarianism," as an authority, for all intents and purposes, that is on par with Scripture. Others view the church's development of biblical doctrines as a helpful guide, but all the while emphasize looking back to the Scriptures as the ultimate authority. Of course, there are some who would refuse to take anything from church history as authoritative in any way.

I want to be up front about my prioritizations when it comes to authority. I view the Bible as the ultimate and highest authority, and one to which all others bow. I view the history of the church and its interpretation as important, vital, helpful, and yet *not* on the same level as Scripture. Christians should always evaluate the decisions of the early church through the lens of Scripture, for only the Bible is inspired and inerrant. So much of the submission conversation has bypassed the Bible for its interpretation in the church, and I think that is a dangerous deviation from what the early church itself would have demanded. Thus, one intent of this

Preface

work is to force the conversation backward from church history to the Scriptures themselves. *Ad fontes*.

Second, I was confronted by the question of where on the spectrum of theological priorities to place the question of the Son's submission. Should this be considered an essential of the Christian faith? If I argue for ESS as an accurate representation of the triune God, should I consider those who disagree to be heretics? This is the severity with which many have approached the issue, evidenced by the harsh tone of accusations of heresy, Arianism, and the like. Personally, I have come to steer away from placing the issue of eternal submission on the level of essentials. While I do consider this to be of great importance in order to more fully understand the triune God, I do not think it is essential for saving faith or even to have an adequate view of God. While I do see the Son's eternal submission in the biblical text, I concede that it is contested, and want to be charitable with others who read these texts differently. At the end of the day, I would consider eternal submission a doctrine necessary neither for faith nor fellowship. I would have no reservations about breaking bread with those who take an alternate view to my own. So, while I am willing to strongly debate and even argue the points made in what follows, I will not consider or accuse those with opposing beliefs of having unorthodox, heretical views. The facet of God's inner life that involves authority and submission is somewhat elusive and mysterious to us, and so believers on both ends of this theological spectrum should use humility when engaging with others of differing opinions here.

The majority of this volume was written as a ThM thesis for Western Seminary in the spring of 2018. Because of the ongoing nature of this discussion, there are several works that have appeared since that time with which I only have limited interaction. I have not attempted a comprehensive approach to addressing all voices within this debate. Instead, I have intentionally chosen to engage with a few whom I consider to be representative of the camps into which they fall. I am certain there are aspects of arguments that need to be expanded, or issues which I have failed to address as thoroughly as they deserve. Perhaps there will be opportunity in the future to more fully develop one or more of these areas.

My hope for this volume is that both proponents and opponents of eternal submission would pick it up and read it carefully, thoughtfully, with an eye on the text of Scripture. As I said above, so much of this debate has focused on the development of Trinitarian doctrine in church history that the biblical sources have largely been neglected. When they are discussed, it is not to exegete them in their own context, but as proof texts toward winning an argument. My first purpose, then, would be to cause both sides in the debate to go back to the only ultimately authoritative source for final guidance in this debate. May both advocates and opponents of ESS submerge themselves deeply in the texts of Scripture that are relevant for this issue.

My second purpose is to perhaps help the pendulum swing back in regard to the eternal submission question. It seems after the blog war of several summers ago that opponents of ESS have been outspoken and successful in gathering numbers to their side. Many seem to consider the war to be finished and the outcome to be the abandonment of any adherence to eternal submission among evangelicals. But is this the reality? Yes, those who have been opposed are outspoken, but the opinions of a few academics in ivory towers do not a church council make nor sound doctrine necessarily determine. And if their conclusions are not reflective of all in evangelicalism, where are the dissenting voices? Surely not everyone has abandoned the position of eternal submission. Why then, to this point, have only a few spoken up to defend it? Perhaps for fear of criticism, or of academic pressures, advocates of the Son's eternal submission have been recently very silent.

As others in this debate have expressed, at the end of the day this is about correctly presenting and explaining the triune God. If that is the case, those who believe, as I do, Scripture teaches that the Son eternally submits to the Father willingly, voluntarily, and lovingly have a moral obligation to speak up for that conviction. I am hopeful that this volume might challenge some who have formerly supported the doctrine of eternal submission and have

Preface

more recently taken a position of silence to regain their voice and reaffirm their support. I hope the issues raised in this book will be picked up on, expanded, and advanced by those who see the doctrine as biblically affirmed and theologically satisfying.

Ultimately, my prayer is that through the effort involved in this publication that the triune God would be magnified, exalted, and glorified among his people as we seek to understand him more clearly. May the eternal Son be worshipped rightly as Almighty God who, from eternity, in voluntary love, submitted himself to his Father to become incarnate in order to redeem and restore lost humanity, who continues to exhibit that eternally submissive disposition while seated at the Father's right hand today, and who, in the unending ages of future human history, will always volitionally subject himself to his Father. "To Him who sits on the throne, and to the Lamb, be blessing and honor and glory and dominion forever and ever," (Rev 5:13).

Acknowledgements

THERE ARE MANY PEOPLE who contributed greatly to this project. Dr. Myron Houghton helped ignite an interest in the triune God that has stayed with me ever since. I am so grateful for his teaching and friendship. Special thanks to the faculty of Western Seminary for their excellent teaching and encouragement of theological development. Thanks to J. Ryan Lister for offering a ThM seminar on the Trinity that renewed old interest in the topic and sparked a world of new possibilities for exploration. Ryan continually offered helpful feedback and pushed me to think further in important areas of this project. Thanks to Patrick Schreiner for his stretching and challenging of many of my preunderstandings related to biblical and theological studies, and for his honest critiques and feedback on this project. I also want to thank Josh Mathews and Todd Miles, who read my thesis and provided helpful responses. Thanks to the many friends I made at Western Seminary, who helped sharpen my thinking in these areas.

I am thankful to the Bible faculty of Emmaus Bible College for their support and contributions to this project. Mark Stevenson and Raju Kunjummen read this manuscript and provided very helpful feedback. Special thanks to Raju for the opportunity to present my thesis topic at a seminar before faculty and students, and for the feedback received after the seminar. I am very grateful to the administration of the college for their encouragement and support throughout my graduate studies and work on this publication. And to the students whose classroom queries and lunchtime

Acknowledgements

conversations assisted in exploring the unfathomable depths of the inner workings of the eternal life of the triune God.

I'm thankful for all my friends and family members who have provided constant love, support, and encouragement throughout this process, and at many points have offered their thoughts on the issues presented herein. To my grandfather, Ray Routley, for the godly example of a life lived in uncompromising devotion to the Lord Jesus Christ and submission to his authority. To my parents, Jon and Mary, for their display of God's love in the home in which I was raised. Thank you to Jonathan Asher and Lillian Janae, my two children, whom I pray would pursue the increase of their knowledge of the triune God with a relentless and insatiable zeal. I am inexpressibly thankful for my wife, Janelle, who not only endured through my long nights of study but encouraged me to research well and glorify the Lord through this project. Without her sacrificial devotion to our family I would not have been able to complete this work. I am forever grateful for her unconditioned love, faithfulness, and joyfulness.

Above all, I want to acknowledge the greatness of my Savior, Jesus Christ, the eternal Son of God, who took on humanity in order to accomplish the redemption of the world and of my corrupted life. May everything that follows only and always bring glory to the only begotten God.

Chapter 1

THE QUESTION OF ETERNAL SUBMISSION

Presentation of the Problem

A MAJOR BATTLE IS raging in evangelicalism today over one sharply debated aspect of Trinitarian theology.[1] All agree that Jesus was submissive to God the Father during his incarnation and time on earth leading to the cross. The issue at hand is whether or not Jesus the Son is *eternally* submissive or subordinate to the Father in terms of their relations. On one side of the debate are those who say that the Son is only subordinate in authority during his earthly ministry, but is coequal, both ontologically and relationally, with the Father eternally. On the other side are those who claim that the Son's obedience and submission during his earthly ministry demonstrates an eternal, voluntary submission to the Father so that the Son is always subordinate relationally while remaining equal with the Father ontologically.

In the modern era, until recently, the former position has been advanced largely by egalitarians.[2] Kevin Giles, a leading voice

---

1. Kevin Giles uses the imagery of this Trinitarian debate as a civil war within evangelicalism. Giles, *Rise and Fall*, 35.

2. Egalitarian is a term that describes a view of women's roles that sees women as equal to men in terms of the offices that they can hold in the church

for this side, has passionately argued that asserting that the Son is eternally subordinate to the Father in role or authority is neither biblically warranted nor sustained by the theology of Trinitarians throughout church history. In fact, he argues, the claim follows and supports Arianism.[3] In the early fourth century AD, Arius and his followers advanced the idea that Jesus as the Son of God was a lesser divine being, not to be fully equated with God the Father. For Giles, the idea that Jesus is eternally subordinate to God the Father in their intra-Trinitarian relationship is contradictory with the statement of the Nicene Creed that the Son is "Light from Light, true God from true God."[4]

In recent years, debate has erupted within the complementarian camp as well, evidenced by the work of Rachel Miller, Amiee Byrd, Liam Goligher, Carl Trueman, and others.[5] These individuals have questioned the biblical and theological validity of asserting that the Son is eternally subordinate to the Father in either authority or role. Their major contention is that in the history of Trinitarian development within the early church, the church fathers do not speak about the Son as submissive to the Father eternally, but only as it relates to redemptive history.[6] Furthermore, they claim that using the eternal subordination of the Son as a way to support gender distinctions within the church and marital relationships is irresponsible and even heretical.[7] Some of these individuals have

---

and level of authority in the home.

3. Giles, "Son of God," 21. Giles, "Doctrine of Trinity," 273.

4. Leith, *Creeds of Churches*, 33. Leith identifies what we commonly refer to as the "Nicene Creed" with the Constatinopolitan Creed of 381.

5. Miller, "Does The Son?"; Goligher, "Is it Okay?"; Trueman, "Fahrenheit 381."

6. Miller, "Does The Son?"

7. Goligher says in reference to proponents of eternal submission: "To speculate, suggest, or say, as some do, that there are three minds, three wills, and three powers with the Godhead is to move beyond orthodoxy (into neo-tritheism) and to verge on idolatry (since it posits a different God). It should certainly exclude such people from holding office in the church of God." Goligher, "Is it Okay?"

The Question of Eternal Submission

recently accused scholars Wayne Grudem and Bruce Ware, among others, of heresy, calling for their resignation from academia.[8]

Thesis, Scope, and Limitations of the Study

Is Jesus the Son eternally submissive to God the Father, in terms of their relations, and why does it matter? This study will argue that Jesus the Son, while ontologically fully God in himself, is eternally relationally submissive to God the Father as evidenced by the witness of Scripture and theological reasoning. The Son's submission is not merely in the economic workings of the triune God, but within their immanent and eternal Trinitarian relationship. The term "Son" used for Jesus throughout the Scriptures not only denotes his eternal generation from the Father, but also his eternal relationship or role corresponding to the Father. This eternal submission has implications for human relationships in that human beings have been created in God's image, and part of that image is relationality.

While many have defended the eternal submission of Jesus to the Father, up until recently, this defense has been mainly expressed against attacks from egalitarian opponents. In light of recent criticisms from within the complementarian camp, what is needed now is first, an assessment of the similarities and differences between the positions of both egalitarian *and* complementarian opponents of eternal submission, and second, a reexamination of eternal submission that takes into account arguments from both opposing positions.

In order to accomplish the purpose listed above, I will begin by clearly defining terminology that is used in discussion of the eternal submission of the Son. Different scholars employ differing terminologies that sometimes overlap and other times contain slight distinctions. Terms and phrases such as the eternal subordination (or submission) of the Son (ES or ESS), eternal functional subordination (EFS), and eternal roles of authority and submission

---

8. See especially Goligher, "Is it Okay?," and Trueman, "Fahrenheit 381."

(ERAS) each bring their own perspective on the discussion to the table. It will be helpful to begin by defining these terms and providing some of the context from which each arose.[9] I will argue below that the "eternal submission of the Son" (ESS) is currently the best terminology to use.

From that initial discussion I will move into an analysis of modern criticisms of ESS. Rather than attempting a comprehensive study of every person who has critiqued ESS, both among egalitarians and complementarians (and there are many), I will focus on a select few who are representative of each. The writings of Kevin Giles will serve as a characteristic cross-section of the egalitarian fountain of opposition to ESS. Giles has led the way in opposing the eternal submission of the Son for over twenty years. There is perhaps no one more strongly opposed to ESS. Recent blogs by Liam Goligher and Carl Trueman will give a representative picture of the opposition rising from the complementarian camp.[10] Goligher and Trueman posted online articles in 2016 that brought this debate to the forefront of evangelicalism. Interacting with these three individuals as conversation partners will provide opportunity to compare and contrast the two perspectives and draw some general conclusions without interacting with the entire spectrum of critics.

Following a discussion of its modern critics and their criticisms, I will move to an examination of ESS from a biblical perspective. For biblical support, I will limit my evaluation to a handful of texts: John 6:38-40, Hebrews 5:4-5, 1 Corinthians 15:24-28, Philippians 2:5-11, Revelation 1:1, and 1 Corinthians 11:3. In John 6:38-40 and Hebrews 5:4-5, I will focus on Christ's submission before his incarnation. Philippians 2:5-11 focuses on

---

9. While there are many variations to this doctrine, for the purposes of this paper I will use the abbreviation ESS as a general reference to the Son's eternal and voluntary submission to his Father in their immanent relations.

10. Although their views are not published in professional journals or books, Goligher and Trueman led the campaign against ESS during the Trinitarian debate of 2016, and so acted as the leaders of the opposition to ESS. To ignore their writings, even though they exist in a somewhat rough form online, would be to ignore a major portion of this current argument.

The Question of Eternal Submission

the relationship between Father and Son prior to, during, and after Jesus' first advent. First Corinthians 15:26-28 and Revelation 1:1 demonstrate the submissive relationship of the Son to the Father after the resurrection and ascension. Finally, 1 Corinthians 11:3 is so often referred to in this discussion that it would be helpful to reexamine and reevaluate that verse.

The following table illustrates the Scriptures that will be reviewed as they relate to the submission of the Son to the Father and the timing of his submission:

Passage	Pre-Incarnation	Incarnate Ministry	Post-Resurrection, Ascension
John 6:38-40	X		
Heb 5:4-5	X		
Phil 2:5-11	X	X	X
1 Cor 15:24-28			X
Rev 1:1			X
1 Cor 11:3			X

Biblical Texts to be Examined on Eternal Submission

Due to the emphasis of this study on the biblical and theological arguments for ESS, I will not attempt to survey the question of eternal submission in church history. Much attention has been given to this discussion in the past year. A thorough study of eternal submission in the theology of the church fathers is beyond the scope of this present study and could easily develop into an extensive study of its own. However, I will examine the history of the church's interpretation in regard to one biblical passage: 1 Corinthians 15:20-28. This brief study will serve to illustrate that the question of eternal submission is not one that will ultimately be decided by an examination of church history.

Having analyzed ESS from biblical and (briefly) historical perspectives, I will move into a theological examination. There are many directions that could be taken in seeking to provide theological support of eternal submission. However, rather than simply provide theological arguments in support of ESS, I will also seek to refute popular theological arguments against the position. Thus, I have attempted to identify several theological arguments against ESS in order to interact with these areas of common critique. I will first discuss the legitimacy of applying submission to the relations of the Trinity, but not to the divine essence. Next, I will examine Rahner's rule that the immanent Trinity is the economic Trinity (and vice versa), and address the issue of whether or not ESS imposes the economic Trinity upon the immanent Trinity. Then I will discuss and refute three common arguments against ESS: the argument from divine simplicity[11] (God is not composed of parts, so how could one divine person submit to another?); the argument from divine immutability (God does not change, therefore if ESS is correct then the Son is essentially or *necessarily* submissive and not *voluntarily* so); and the argument concerning the inseparable operations of the Trinitarian persons (one divine person does not act independently of the other, so if one submits, don't all submit?). Finally, I will examine the question of whether eternal generation necessitates eternal submission from the Son to the Father.

I will conclude by examining the implications of this study for our understanding of the Trinity and human relationships. If Jesus the Son eternally submits to his Father in their divine relationship, and human beings have been created in God's image, what does this mean (and what does it *not* mean) for how we think about the triune God and humanity?

Toward a Definition of Eternal Submission

What exactly is eternal submission, and how has it been defined by those who have advocated for its biblical basis? These questions are important to explore at the outset so that a clear definition can be presented and used consistently throughout the study. While it would be impractical to survey all definitions of eternal subordination that have been advanced in the past forty years, a short

---

11. The issue of the divine will is to be examined at this point as well, which has been a key ingredient in this theological discussion.

survey of the subject as discussed by several of its proponents will be most helpful.

Eternal Functional Subordination: Wayne Grudem

In his *Systematic Theology*, Grudem advocates for the eternal subordination of the Son (and the Spirit) to the Father in role and function.[12] In speaking of the separate roles of the Father and Son, Grudem says that, while they are equal, they have "different functions or primary activities" in relation to the world which display an eternal distinction.[13] So in creation God decrees, the Son carries out the decrees, the Spirit works by "sustaining and manifesting God's immediate presence in his creation."[14] The Son functions in a way that is subordinate to the Father (although he is ontologically equal) in that the Father possesses the authority of initiating in the work of creation, and the Son is the one through whom all things are created.[15]

These functions are indicative of the eternal roles of triune persons. Grudem categorizes the functions of the Father, Son, and Spirit as follows:

> We may say that the role of the Father in creation and redemption has been to plan and direct and send the Son and Holy Spirit. This is not surprising, for it shows that the Father and the Son relate to one another as a father and son relate to one another in a human family: the father directs and has authority over the son, and the son obeys and is responsive to the directions of the father. The Holy Spirit is obedient to the directives of both the Father and the Son.[16]

---

12. Grudem, *Systematic Theology*, 248–56.
13. Grudem, *Systematic Theology*, 248, 250–51.
14. Grudem, *Systematic Theology*, 248.
15. Grudem, "Biblical Evidence," 243.
16. Grudem, *Systematic Theology*, 249.

Eternal Submission

He goes on to argue that these differences in role are not exclusive to the way God deals with creation alone, but reflect an eternal distinction in the relationships between the divine persons. "The different functions that we see the Father, Son, and Holy Spirit performing are simply outworkings of an eternal relationship between the three persons, one that has always existed and will exist for eternity."[17] Grudem goes so far as to say, "If the Son is not eternally subordinate to the Father in role, then the Father is not eternally 'Father' and the Son is not eternally 'Son.' This would mean that the Trinity has not eternally existed."[18]

Kevin Giles, who opposes eternal subordination, has called Grudem's discussion of the topic in his *Systematic Theology* the most developed expression of the Son's subordination.[19] Certainly, with the popularity of Grudem's work, it can be said this is one of the strongest influences in advocating on behalf of the Son's role of subordination. Grudem does not have any problem using the term "subordination" in referring to the Son, although in more recent writings, he opts for use of "submission" instead.[20] Ultimately, he does not see a major difference in the use of the two terms, and spends some time defending the use of "subordination" as descriptive of the Son's role in the immanent Trinity.[21]

From Grudem's survey we are introduced to the language of subordination in terms of functions and roles. The subordination of the Son is sometimes termed *eternal functional subordination* to denote the Son's subordination in terms of his actions as opposed to his being. Thus, the Son could be called equal in being or nature, but subordinate in act or function, which coincides with his role as Son. Grudem, then, sets the foundation for an understanding of eternal submission.

---

17. Grudem, *Systematic Theology*, 250.
18. Grudem, *Systematic Theology*, 251.
19. Giles, *Trinity*, 83.
20. See especially Grudem, "Biblical Evidence," 224. See also Grudem, "Doctrinal Deviations."
21. Grudem, "Biblical Evidence," 225.

The Question of Eternal Submission

Eternal Relational Authority-Submission: Bruce Ware

Bruce Ware's *Father, Son, & Holy Spirit: Relationships, Roles, and Relevance* has also done much to advance the eternal subordination of the Son at the popular level.[22] Ware builds on Grudem's understanding of the functions and roles of the Trinitarian persons by focusing on their eternal relationships. He places the Son eternally under the headship or authority of the Father, based on 1 Corinthians 11:3.[23] For Ware, this passage is not only referring to the incarnation, but the eternal relationships of the Father and the Son.

One of Ware's contributions to the discussion is his analysis of the term *taxis*, used by the early church to speak of the ordering of the three Trinitarian persons within the immanent Trinity.[24] This order, or *taxis*, is part of the eternal distinction between the Father, Son, and Spirit. Ware writes, "Intrinsic to God's own nature is a fundamental *taxis*, and he has so designed creation to reflect his own being, his own internal and eternal relationships, in part, through created and designed relationships of *taxis*."[25] Thus, the ordering of the persons in the Trinity reveals a structure of authority and submission that is reflected throughout Scripture, but explicit in 1 Corinthians 11:3.

Ware argues that Jesus' submission to the Father in the economy of salvation was a reflection of his eternal submission. He looks closely at the correspondence in John's Gospel between John's portrayal of Jesus as the divine Son of God and Jesus' submission to his Father. In John 8, for example, Ware says:

> The very same Jesus who claims implicitly to be God (John 8:23) then proceeds to describe himself as doing nothing by his own authority, speaking only what the Father teaches him, and doing only and always what pleases the Father (vv. 28–29). How amazing this is. Jesus

---

22. Ware, *Father, Son.*
23. Ware, *Father, Son,* 72.
24. Ware, *Father, Son,* 72–73.
25. Ware, *Father, Son,* 72.

Eternal Submission

is God, but Jesus obeys God . . . Clearly, the only way to make sense of this is to see that the eternal Son of the Father is both "*God* the Son" and "God the *Son.*" That is, as eternally divine and not of this world, he is *God* the Son, but as under the authority of his Father, and as the eternal Son of the Father, he is God the *Son.* Both are true of Christ, and that both are true is a wonder indeed.[26]

In addition to looking at the human life of Christ in John for evidence of an eternal submission of the Son to the Father, Ware finds support in other locations as well. First Corinthians 11:3 supports his view that humanity bears an ordering (*taxis*) of authority and submission that reflects the divine ordering between Father and Son.[27] He sees the sending of the Son by the Father in John's Gospel as evidence of the eternal roles of authority and submission.[28] First Peter 1:18–21 also shows, for Ware, the roles of authority and submission "in which the Father chooses and sends, and the Son submits and comes."[29] First Corinthians 15 shows the submission of the Son to the Father extending into the eternal future.[30]

Ware's contributions to a definition of eternal submission are important. Whereas Grudem focuses on the economic functions of the Trinitarian persons as indicative of their eternal roles, Ware narrows in on biblical support for the eternal relationship between Father and Son as the proper area for discussion of authority and submission.[31] In doing this, he guards more carefully than Grudem against accusations of reading the economic Trinity back into the immanent Trinity. Ware is also much more hesitant to use

---

26. Ware, *Father, Son*, 74. See also Ware, "Equal in Essence," 20.

27. Ware, *Father, Son*, 77.

28. Ware, *Father, Son*, 77–78. Ware cites John 3:16–17; 10:36; 6:38; 8:28 as clear examples of the Father sending the Son prior to the Son's incarnation.

29. Ware, *Father, Son*, 79.

30. Ware, *Father, Son*, 83–84.

31. Grudem, to be sure, includes biblical support in his presentation of eternal subordination. Yet much of his biblical support argues from the economic relations of Father and Son backward to the eternal life of God. Ware seems more interested to find biblical passages that focus primarily on the eternal.

the term "subordination," preferring "submission" to describe the relationship of Son's obedience to the Father. Perhaps he recognizes the problems and confusion generated by the use of the term "subordination."

Eternal Voluntary Submission: Robert Letham[32]

Robert Letham has much to offer in constructing a definition of eternal submission. Letham expresses the importance of not arguing from human relationships back into the immanent Trinity, not viewing the Trinity as a hierarchy (no rank among the Godhead), and warning against the very use of the term "subordination" at all in reference to the Son based on negative historical connotations.[33]

At the same time, Letham believes the Son's obedience to the Father in the economy of salvation reflects a greater immanent reality. In pointing to the Son's preincarnate sending from the Father, Letham says, "His sending preceded his incarnation and so his incarnate life and ministry can (as appropriate) reveal something of his eternal relations. If this were not so, we would be left with agnosticism, in flat contradiction to Jesus' own words that he who has seen him (in his lowliness) has seen the Father (John 14:9 et al.)."[34] Jesus fully and perfectly reveals the Father, and so his relationship with the Father demonstrated in his humanity must be an accurate portrayal of their relationship in the immanent Trinity.

Second, Letham argues that opponents of eternal subordination[35] do not fully appreciate the implications of the incarnation. Where some make a sharp distinction between the Son incarnate and the Son eternal, Letham conversely points out that Jesus'

---

32. While Robert Letham has argued positively in support of eternal submission in the past, presently he takes a more negative position on ESS. See Giles, *Rise and Fall*, 41–43.

33. Letham, *Holy Trinity*, 490.

34. Letham, "Trinity and Subordinationism," 386.

35. Letham has primarily debated with Kevin Giles on the topic of eternal submission. See bibliography under "Giles" and "Letham" for a thorough listing of their exchange.

Eternal Submission

divine and human nature should be viewed as complementary rather than contradictory. "The incarnation is not some singularity. It is not a temporary expedient simply for the purpose of securing salvation. Christ's humanity is compatible with his divine person and thus congruent with him."[36] Letham says that for the opposing view to be right there would have to be a "kenosis of deity in the incarnation and a similar kenosis of humanity at the resurrection."[37] Christ's humanity is permanent, and since human beings must rely continually in dependence on God, Christ continues in a state of submission to God's will and authority.[38] Those who deny eternal submission, therefore, do not adequately appreciate the doctrine of the hypostatic union.

Third, Letham asks whether functional differentiation demands ontological subordination. He answers by saying:

> The Son's self-emptying, his seeking the interests of the other in his incarnate ministry, is not alien to who God is. This is what God is like. The Son freely chose to become man. He did not regard his equality with God as something to be exploited. His actions recorded in the gospels mirrored his determination in eternity; they were far from incongruous.[39]

For Letham, the Son's submission to the Father does not in any way imply an ontological subordination, but rather demonstrates the *free* and *voluntary* action of the Son that "tells us something vital about the Son and about God Himself."[40]

Fourth, in responding to Kevin Giles[41] on the question of eternal submission, Letham accuses Giles of neglecting Eastern Trinitarian theologians on the matter. He says sharply, "Giles is trapped in the trinitarian paradigm of the Western church."[42] By

---

36. Letham, "Reply to Kevin Giles," 343.
37. Letham, "Reply to Kevin Giles," 343.
38. Letham, "Does the Son?," 13–14.
39. Letham, "Reply to Kevin Giles," 344.
40. Letham, "Does the Son?," 14.
41. Giles' views on eternal submission will be examined in chapter 2 below.
42. Letham, *Holy Trinity*, 493.

The Question of Eternal Submission

contrast, Eastern theologians have long recognized the Father as the fountain of life in the Godhead and stressed his authoritative primacy. "Giles makes a few cursory references to Easterners . . . but shows little interest in their perspective. This is not surprising, since the Eastern stress on the Father as the *Arche* would not strengthen his case at all."[43] Letham also criticizes Giles for his lumping of all contemporary Trinitarian theologians into one group bent on the removal of any form of subordinationism. Letham argues that current scholarship "is far from monolithic."[44]

Last, Letham posits that if egalitarians seriously reflect on Romans 5:12–21, it will overturn their case for mutual reciprocity between genders, and thus they would have no problem seeing submission between the Father and Son. He writes:

> If they [Adam and Eve] were created in a state of complete mutual reciprocity, exactly to the liking of the white, middle-class, educated, liberal-minded, early twenty-first century intelligentsia, why does Paul say that all sinned *in Adam*? If the sin of Adam affects the whole race, if also affected Eve. If it affected Eve, then Adam was in some way her head and representative.[45]

Letham implies some wish to impose their egalitarian understanding of roles and authority, not only into the original created order of man and woman, but back from there into the Godhead itself.

What does Robert Letham contribute to defining eternal submission? First, he explains why the term "subordination" should be avoided in any Trinitarian discussion at all costs. Given the history of the term in its association with ontological subordination and the Arian heresy, scholars should reject the use of such a term. It is unhelpful, confusing, and unnecessarily complicates the discussion. Second, his explanation of the submission of Christ as voluntary and relating to the persons in distinction from the divine essence is one of the keys to this discussion. Christ does not submit because he *has* to, as though the Father forces him into

---

43. Letham, "Trinity and Subordinationism," 385.
44. Letham, "Trinity and Subordinationism," 385.
45. Letham, *Holy Trinity*, 495–96.

subservience. The Son submits because he is eternally disposed toward voluntarily submitting himself to the Father.[46] It is what makes him uniquely God the Son. Those who oppose the eternal submission of the Son are often zealous for the one divine essence, but less concerned about maintaining Trinitarian distinctions.

Evaluation and Proposed Definition

What conclusions can be drawn from this brief study of three leading advocates for eternal submission? First, each of the authors mentioned above desires to maintain the ontological equality of the divine persons: each affirm that Father, Son, and Holy Spirit are fully God. At the same time, in their relationships with one another, there are distinctions related to an order or structure among the persons, so that the Father has authority in the order and the Son, to some degree, submits and obeys. Each scholar cited above, in one way or another, sees a connection between the life of the Son and his submission during his incarnation with his life in eternity. Thus, what the Son does in his humanity is a true and reliable reflection of his divinity. Subordination is a term with so much ecclesio-historical baggage[47] that we should move away from its use and instead substitute submission, which is a more accurate reflection of the Son's relationship to his Father. Finally, the Son's volition in submitting to his Father eternally is of the utmost significance.

These conclusions can help us construct a working definition or description of eternal submission in relation to the Son. The submission of the Son to the Father describes the continuous, ongoing disposition of the second person of the Trinity to voluntarily submit himself to the relational authority of his Father within their intra-Trinitarian relations. The Son's submission is continuous in

---

46. Letham, "Does the Son?," 12

47. By "ecclesio-historical baggage" I am referring to the association between the term "subordination" and the idea that Christ is somehow less than the Father in his deity, demonstrated in the Arian controversy of the fourth century AD.

The Question of Eternal Submission

that it is an eternal status or disposition; he *always* submits to the Father's authority and does what pleases the Father. The Son's submission is voluntary in that it is what he always prefers; no one forces him to submit. The Son's submission is relational in that he is ontologically equal to the Father, yet relationally he takes a submissive position voluntarily. Although the Son fully possesses the divine nature in the same way as Father and Spirit, in terms of their relationships, the Son always submits to and obeys the Father. There is a consistency in the life of the eternal Son so that his relationship with his Father during his incarnation is a true and accurate reflection of their eternal relationship with one another. These points are foundational for the discussion of this study. In the pages that follow, any reference to the eternal submission of the Son will have in mind the definition presented above.

Chapter 2

The Opposition to Eternal Submission

There have been a handful of outspoken egalitarian opponents to eternal submission in the past twenty years since its popularization.[1] During the summer of 2016 the debate exploded within the complementarian camp. Rather than attempt to overview all of the participants in this debate and their views, this chapter will focus on Kevin Giles as representative of egalitarian opposition to ESS, and Liam Goligher and Carl Trueman as representative of complementarian opposition. At the conclusion of the chapter, some comparisons will be drawn between the viewpoints of these representatives.

Egalitarian Opposition: Kevin Giles

Kevin Giles, an Australian Anglican minister, has been one of the leading voices against eternal submission for the past twenty years.[2] Giles adamantly defends the position that the Son is only

---

1. The two most prominent have been Giles and Erickson. See Giles, *Trinity & Subordinationism*; Erickson, *Who's Tampering?*

2. For a survey of his work, see Giles, *Trinity & Subordinationism*; also Giles, *Eternal Generation*.

The Opposition to Eternal Submission

temporally subordinated to the Father during his earthly ministry until the time of his resurrection and ascension.[3] He is not in *any way* subordinate in eternity, especially not, as many evangelicals argue, in authority or role. There are essentially three major arguments that Giles uses throughout his writings to support this position. ESS is in opposition to orthodox Christian tradition, is biblically unwarranted, and is theologically inconsistent.

First, Giles advocates that ESS stands in opposition to orthodox Christian church tradition. He proposes that the idea that the Son is eternally subordinate to the Father in function, authority, or role is a new idea in evangelicalism as of the 1970s.[4] Giles repeatedly asserts that prior to George W. Knight III's writing in 1977, the idea of basing women's subordination in the church and home on the submissive relations in the Trinity was nonexistent.[5] Giles' point is that "the doctrine of an eternally subordinated Son in function and authority is found only in post 1970s conservative evangelical writings. It is unknown in mainline Protestant and Roman Catholic works on the Trinity."[6] He gives credit for the rise of this doctrine to George Knight III, Wayne Grudem, and Bruce Ware among others.[7] For Giles, Grudem's *Systematic Theology* has done the most to advance this teaching in evangelicalism with its widespread popularity.[8]

Furthermore, Giles sees eternal functional subordination as akin to the Arian heresy. Giles looks back at the fourth century debate and comments that not only did the Arians believe Christ to be of a lesser nature than the Father, they also subordinated him in terms of authority.[9] "What is of some surprise to many is

---

3. Giles, "Doctrine of Trinity," 281.

4. Giles, *Jesus and Father*, 20.

5. Giles, "Evangelical Theological Society," 324. See also Giles, *The Trinity & Subordinationism*, 83.

6. Giles, "Evangelical Theological Society," 325–26. See also Giles, *Eternal Generation*, 228–31.

7. Giles, "Defining Error," 219–20.

8. Giles, *Jesus and Father*, 21–22.

9. Giles, *Jesus and Father*, 87.

Eternal Submission

that for the Arians this ontological subordination *always* had as its corollary the eternal functional subordination of the Son."[10] He goes on to state that Athanasius explicitly argued against the Arians on these points as well as in making the Son a lesser god. Giles sees a consistency in the tradition of the church of viewing Christ as subordinate only in relation to his humanity and never in his deity, in contrast to what the Arians asserted.[11] Thus, Giles argues that if the Son is eternally submissive to the Father, he is also *necessarily* submissive.[12]

Giles calls the Cappadocian fathers, Augustine, Calvin, Barth, Rahner, and others to testify to the orthodoxy of his position.[13] In his book *The Trinity & Subordinationism*, Giles has both a chapter outlining those who have opposed all forms of subordinationism, and a chapter showing where individuals and groups have veered away from this view to allow for some type of heretical subordinationism in the Godhead.[14] He critiques his opponents' reading of church history as biased, saying, "They turn to the Bible, the historical sources, and the writings of modern theologians simply to find comments that would support what they already believe or to refute their critics."[15]

This helps to explain why, for Giles, the stakes in this discussion are so high. Those who deny ESS stand in the orthodox tradition of the church in opposition to heresy that threatens to undermine the very doctrine of God.[16] He believes that the eternal submission argument is used wrongly to advance teaching re-

---

10. Giles, "Doctrine of Trinity," 273.

11. Giles, *Jesus and Father*, 87.

12. Giles, *Jesus and Father*, 59. Giles says, "I argue that to teach that the Son must always obey the Father, that he is eternally subordinated in authority to the Father, also implies his ontological subordination. If the Son must always obey the Father, he is not the Father's equal in power." Giles, *Jesus and Father*, 59.

13. Giles, *Jesus and Father*, 82–90.

14. Giles, *Trinity & Subordinationism*, 32–105.

15. Giles, *Jesus and Father*, 91. Giles does not appear to realize that the same accusation could be leveled against him in his use of church history.

16. Giles, *Trinity & Subordinationism*, 106–9.

garding male headship in the church and home. In his judgment, the ecclesiological desires of complementarians who use ESS to support male headship and female submission are steering their theological thoughts regarding the Son's submission.[17] This issue, then, has direct implications not only for our understanding of God but also our understanding of the church and of the marriage relationship.

Second, Giles asserts that ESS is biblically fallacious. In his interpretation of biblical texts he relies heavily on Augustine in seeing the Son in the immanent Trinity as being in "the form of God" and in his humanity as "the form of a servant."[18] This informs his reading of all NT texts that could be used to advance the functional subordination of the Son. In commenting on John 14:28, for example, he writes, "This is a difficult text to be sure because it stands in stark contrast to John's teaching that the Son reveals the Father and the Father and the Son are one. The best solution would seem to be that given by Ambrose, Augustine, Calvin and many others that Jesus here speaks as the incarnate Son in his state of humiliation."[19]

Giles' exegesis of Philippians 2:5–11 yields evidence of Jesus' equality with the Father and willful humility in taking on humanity. He speaks repeatedly of Christ's voluntarily taking on humanity, while at the same time asserting, "There is no hint here of a Son eternally subordinated to the Father in being, function, or authority. Instead there is a bold revelation of the Father and the Son reciprocally related in giving and receiving, ruling and serving."[20] Thus, Philippians 2:5–11 supports the eternal equality of the Son with the Father and his temporal submission during his incarnation.[21]

---

17. Giles, *Trinity & Subordinationism*, 109. The same accusation in reverse, however, might be leveled against Giles as well here.

18. Giles, *Jesus and Father*, 85.

19. Giles, "Doctrine of Trinity," 283.

20. Giles, *Jesus and Father*, 103.

21. For the full discussion of this passage see Giles, *Jesus and Father*, 100–3.

Eternal Submission

His discussion of 1 Corinthians 11:3 and 15:28 is also significant. In the former, Giles does not see a four-tiered hierarchy but instead "a three-fold pairing: in each case one person being the metaphorical head of another, and not in a hierarchical order."[22] He claims the passage is about maintaining gender distinctions between men and women rather than maintaining a Trinity-inspired order. In 1 Corinthians 15:28, Giles advocates for a mutual reciprocity between the Father and the Son as the Son reigns after his resurrection until he hands the kingdom back to the Father. "Rather than speaking of fixed roles, or of the eternal subordination of the Son, this text indicates a changing of roles in differing epochs."[23]

There are also times when Giles advocates for the use of Second Temple Jewish understandings in interpreting certain texts. In John's Gospel, for example, discussion of Jesus being sent by the Father should be read in light of the Jewish concept of *Shaliach*. "In Judaism the one sent (the *Shaliach*) has the same authority as the one who sends him: he is as the sender himself."[24] Thus, when we read that the Father sent the Son (John 8:42; 17:3, 23), this must be understood from a first-century Jewish perspective primarily and not from our modern culturally-conditioned perspective.[25]

Third, eternal submission is theologically inconsistent. Giles argues there is really no difference between saying the Son is eternally subordinate in *role* and that he is eternally subordinate in *essence, being,* or *nature*. This is one of Giles' key arguments that is repeated throughout his writings over the past decade. If one says that the Son is eternally subordinate to the Father in role or function, this means that He is "*necessarily* subordinate" and so *must* obey the Father. For Giles, the implication is that if the Son has no choice but to obey eternally, he is not truly one with the Father. Instead he is *essentially* or *ontologically* subordinated.[26]

22. Giles, *Jesus and Father*, 283.
23. Giles, *Jesus and Father*, 284.
24. Giles, *Jesus and Father*, 119.
25. Giles, *Jesus and Father*, 119.
26. Giles, "Defining Error," 222.

The Opposition to Eternal Submission

Additionally, while Giles does not want to see any form of eternal submission in reference to the Son, he does hold to the eternal generation of the Son. The question that follows is whether or not eternal generation demands eternal submission. In his response, Giles asserts that eternal generation is not like the human act of generation from which one being is produced by another, and so the Father is neither ontologically greater nor greater in rank or authority than the Son as relates to the persons in the imminent Trinity.[27] For Giles, eternal generation is the orthodox doctrine of the church, but it does not imply any form of subordination.

Kevin Giles' arguments are thorough and extensive. For Giles, the witness of church tradition, the witness of the Scriptures, and the witness of theological reasoning all point to the conclusion that the Son cannot be submissive to the Father in any eternal sense, but only in relation to his humanity. For the Son to be submissive to the Father eternally, even if he chooses to act in this way, demands that he is ontologically inferior, and thus not equal to the Father.

Complementarian Opposition

Liam Goligher and Carl Trueman have likewise argued that the eternal subordination of the Son to the Father is a deviation from historical Trinitarian theology. These men, unlike Giles, have identified (at least until very recently) as complementarian rather than egalitarian.[28] However they do not agree with complementarians who attempt to support their claims by citing Jesus' submission in the Trinity. In Goligher's words, likening the relationship between husband and wife to the Father and Son in eternity fails "to distinguish between God as He is in Himself (ontology) and God as He is in Christ in [the] outworking of the plan of redemption (economy)."[29] Thus, they make a sharp distinction between God's

---

27. Giles, *Eternal Generation*, 219.
28. Goligher, "Is it Okay?"
29. Goligher, "Is it Okay?"

life in eternity and God's life in redemptive history, or between the immanent and the economic Trinity.

Liam Goligher

Senior Minister of Tenth Presbyterian Church in Philadelphia Liam Goligher argues that complementarians who attempt to read ESS into the Trinity "are following the egalitarians in redefining the Triune nature of God to defend their position."[30] Just as egalitarians wrongly understand the nature of God, ESS-supporting complementarians wrongly understand God's nature as well. Goligher views these individuals as departing from classical Christian orthodoxy and moving toward idolatry in their false representations of God.[31] His argumentation focuses on two areas: ESS is fallacious from both ecclesio-historical and biblical-theological perspectives.

First, Goligher contends that ESS separates from classical Christian orthodoxy in its understanding of the oneness and unity of the triune God. Goligher emphasizes that although there are three persons in the Godhead, they share one common divine nature. This seems to be the driving factor behind much of his argumentation. For Goligher, it appears the immanent Trinity must be viewed primarily from the vantage point of the divine essence.

> These eternal relations, absolutely considered, pertain to being: the Son and Spirit share the very nature of God as God—they are essentially identical (though relatively distinct). Within this eternal life, there was distinction without primacy and order of being without priority of life or authority. The Father is God, the Son is God, and the Spirit is God. There is only one God and we baptize in the threefold name of that one God.[32]

---

30. Goligher, "Is it Okay?"
31. Goligher, "Reinventing God."
32. Goligher, "Is it Okay?"

The Opposition to Eternal Submission

Goligher's view of the Trinity begins with the one divine nature and then proceeds to the three persons, but the one nature is primary. As we saw in the first chapter, this reflects a Western approach to understanding the Trinity, whereas an Eastern approach places more emphasis on the three persons.[33]

For Goligher, the creeds and confessions of Christian orthodoxy highlight the oneness of God and carefully guard against misrepresentations of his relationality:

> In that eternal repose there was one mind, one will, one love, one power shared equally by the divine persons in perfect unity and identity of being. It is in this contemplation of God that I need both the Bible and the language of the church. I need the carefully crafted words of the church's creeds to keep me from misunderstanding God or misrepresenting Him. In this regard what one or two theologians said about God in the 350's AD while debates were going on, is not as important as what is found in the ecumenical creeds like the Nicene-Constantinople Creed of 381 AD.[34]

Thus, while the Bible is authoritative, the church's interpretation of the Bible as expressed in its creeds and confessions is a necessary guidepost for understanding the Trinity. Those creeds and confessions strongly emphasize divine unity yet are silent on distinctions in eternal roles or functions.

If the divine persons are not distinguished by their roles of authority and submission in the creeds, how are they distinguished? Goligher points to eternal generation and procession, or spiration, as the distinguishing features of the persons in the Godhead.

> The Father is unbegotten; the Son is begotten and the Holy Spirit proceeds from the Father and the Son. The personal names of "Father," "Son," and "Spirit" refer to

---

33. Letham, *Holy Trinity,* 493. Letham accuses Kevin Giles similarly, saying, "Giles is trapped in the Trinitarian paradigm of the Western church. Augustine found some difficulty in doing justice to the three, in particular to the Holy Spirit. The West since has found this even more difficult." Letham, *Holy Trinity,* 493.

34. Goligher, "Dr. Liam Goligher Responds."

relations of *origin* rather than relations of *authority* (we must not read human paternity back into divine paternity; much less human patriarchy back into the eternal God, for He is not altogether like us).[35]

Goligher critiques Grudem sharply on this point:

> The real problem with the position as represented by Grudem, for example, is that they deny the classical hypostatic differentiation of the Son as eternally begotten and the Spirit as eternally proceeding. Therefore, to avoid modalism, they must talk about eternal submission or subordination.[36]

Thus, ESS advocates also deviate from historic orthodoxy by replacing eternal generation with eternal submission in their discussion of the eternal distinctives of the divine persons.

Second, Goligher's emphasis on the unity of God leads him to argue that ESS is theologically inconsistent with God's nature. His theological argumentation, similar to and stemming from his historical argumentation, begins with the unity of God as its starting point. This leads him to contend that ESS cannot be reconciled with divine simplicity, inseparable divine operations, one divine will, and God's self-revelation. Each of these points will be briefly examined.

Goligher asserts that eternal submission destroys divine simplicity by, in effect, creating three separate parts or components of God which act differently. "The eternal subordination of the Son challenges the simplicity of God. The very ideas of functions and roles within the Trinity ad intra are inconceivable, they are subsistent relations fully in act."[37] Simplicity, then, is related to the inseparable operations, or works of God. Goligher speaks of the works of God as stemming from his divine will. Creation and redemption, therefore, were both an act of each of the persons according to one divine will. Goligher goes on to explain:

---

35. Goligher, "A Letter to Professors."
36. Goligher, "Dr. Liam Goligher Responds."
37. Goligher, "Dr. Liam Goligher Responds."

The Opposition to Eternal Submission

> This one act of willing and doing occurred simply and immediately without any effort whatsoever on God's part—the inseparable operation of the persons: Father, Son (Word) and Spirit. In the Triune God the three "persons" think as one, will as one, rule as one and act as one, and God does so from the perfect rest of His eternal life.[38]

Because this is true, the idea that the Son eternally submits to the Father clashes with and even undermines their mutual interworking. ESS negates both divine simplicity and inseparable operations.

ESS also challenges the historic view of one divine will. Goligher says, "The will of the Trinity is one will, and the operations of the Trinity are inseparable and indivisible. There is no hierarchy; and there are not three centers of consciousness."[39] Eternal submission demands an eternal will of the Father as well as separate wills of the Son and Spirit, which contradicts the unity expressed in orthodox Christianity. Goligher also explains the difficulty in reconciling the relationship between one divine will and the covenant of redemption:

> Does the idea of the pactum militate against God's one will? Not if we can agree that the one Triune will decreed there would be something external to Himself and that in this external reality (the economy) His will be enacted according to the 'tripersonal manner of subsistence' (Allen & Swain, Christian Dogmatics, 122) within the Trinity.[40]

The covenant of redemption, then, is not an exception to the creedal expression of one divine will, but a qualification of that will.[41]

Finally, God's self-revelation in Christ is misunderstood by supporters of ESS. When it comes to the correspondence of the immanent and economic relationships between Father and Son,

---

38. Goligher, "Is it Okay?"
39. Goligher, "A Letter to Professors."
40. Goligher, "A Letter to Professors."
41. For further discussion of God's one will and ESS, see chapter 6 below.

Eternal Submission

Goligher states that Christ's human life gives us an incomplete picture of what God is like in eternity. "The incarnate Christ sets an example of godly living as God in human flesh; He does not give us an example of the eternal life of God."[42] He also says, "Though God cannot be known in His fullness, yet we can know Him by special revelation; we may know Him truly but not fully."[43] To view Christ as showcasing God in his entirety, then, is to "collapse the intra-trinitarian life of God into the roles adopted by the persons to accomplish our redemption."[44] Advocates of ESS overstep, Goligher argues, by reading the economic relationship between Father and Son back into the eternal life of the triune God.

Carl Trueman

Carl Trueman adds to this discussion by strongly asserting that belief in the eternal subordination of the Son is an anti-Nicene position, and one contrary to the Christian faith throughout the history of the church. He claims that this "new subordinationism" is "a position seriously out of step with the historic catholic faith and a likely staging post to Arianism."[45] Trueman says in no uncertain terms that aligning with ESS places one "not simply outside of the boundaries of the consensus of the confessions of Reformation Protestantism but also outside what has historically been considered orthodox Christianity in its broadest sense."[46]

Trueman's discussion is much narrower than Goligher or Giles. His contention that ESS is unorthodox has its primary focal point in what he terms "Nicene Trinitarianism."[47] For Trueman, eternal submission goes against the Trinitarianism of the Council of Constantinople in 381 in changing the way the relations between

---

42. Goligher, "Is it Okay?"
43. Goligher, "A Letter to Professors."
44. Goligher, "Is it Okay?"
45. Trueman, "Fahrenheit 381."
46. Trueman, "Fahrenheit 381."
47. For examples of this see Trueman, "A Rejoinder"; Trueman, "A Surrejoinder"; and Trueman, "Once More."

The Opposition to Eternal Submission

the Trinitarian persons are represented. "I simply state that those who get rid of eternal generation and speak of eternal submission are outside of the bounds set by 381—which is the ecumenical standard of the church catholic."[48] Trueman elevates this Nicene Trinitarianism expressed by the Council of Constantinople as the standard of orthodox Trinitarian thought, and eternal generation is the key area of deviation.

Grudem and Ware, the leading proponents of ESS, have until very recently questioned or denied the validity of the eternal generation of the Son.[49] Trueman views this as a fatal move, for removing this point from the creed and attempting to replace it with eternal submission deviates from orthodoxy into heresy. He says, "If you argue for EFS and/or reject (or even regard as negotiable) eternal generation,[50] then you stand outside the bounds of the historic Nicene Christian faith as set forth at Constantinople in 381 and held thereafter by the church catholic."[51] Eternal generation, and not submission, is the Trinitarian distinctive affirmed by the orthodox Catholic Church.

While eternal generation is the primary point of deviation for Trueman, there are other implicit areas of diversion.

> Nicene Trinitarianism involves a host of commitments—to divine simplicity as classically articulated by Gregory Nazianzus, to the unity of the divine will, to inseparable operations and, of course, to eternal generation. Repudiation or revision of any one or more of these involves a revision of the whole and thus ceases to be Nicene Trinitarianism.[52]

---

48. Trueman, "A Rejoinder."
49. Giles, *Rise and Fall*, 45.
50. See Grudem, *Systematic Theology*, 1233–34; Ware, *Father, Son*, 162 n. 3 for examples. It seems to this author that Grudem and Ware, rather than blatantly rejecting eternal generation, were skeptical in the past but have now affirmed the doctrine: Giles, *Rise and Fall*, 45.
51. Trueman, "Motivated by Feminism?"
52. Trueman, "A Surrejoinder."

Goligher and Trueman therefore see eye to eye on important theological areas where ESS misses the mark of Nicene Trinitarianism. These theological areas focus on a concern for the unity of the divine essence, aside from the distinctive of eternal generation.

All of these considerations lead Trueman to assert that advocacy of eternal submission pushes one from orthodoxy to heresy. Trueman's concerns with ESS are primarily from a credo-confessional perspective. On this point he yields the authority of church tradition to the Bible, while maintaining a high view of the authority of the creeds. "The creedal tradition is of course corrigible in light of scripture; but one must first understand that tradition in its fulness [sic] and its depth before one declares it to be inadequate or wrong or irrelevant or confusing."[53] Thus church tradition is not to be forsaken lightly.

Egalitarian and Complementarian Opposition Compared and Contrasted

What can be said in analysis of these three critiques of ESS? It is striking to see the similarities in theological argumentation between the egalitarian position and the anti-ESS complementarian position. Both assert that ESS is a novel idea, foreign to the history of the church, and in opposition to the teaching of the early church fathers and classic church creeds and confessions. Both operate from the starting point of emphasizing the oneness or unity of God, a historic point of emphasis in the Western church, following Augustine. Both interpret relevant biblical texts as distinguishing between Christ "in the form of God" and "in the form of a servant," or making a clear distinction between economic Trinitarian relations and immanent relations. Both assert that our understanding of the relationships between men and women in the home and church should not be read backward into the immanent life of God.

Giles by far represents the most thorough opposition to ESS over an extended period of time. Thus, his arguments are probably

---

53. Trueman, "Motivated by Feminism?"

The Opposition to Eternal Submission

the most carefully outlined. What is interesting is that he has focused his argumentation primarily on providing evidence of ESS's departure from orthodox Christianity and showing its lack of biblical support. While Giles has argued certain theological points, these have not been the primary emphasis of his writings. Giles' writings also betray a leaning toward placing emphasis on the oneness of God to the detriment of doing justice to his threeness, which will be further evidenced below.

Goligher and Trueman also argue against the orthodoxy of ESS, but go farther than Giles, however, in theological areas like divine simplicity, inseparable operations, the divine will, and eternal generation. These concerns, both historical and theological, show a leaning toward defending the oneness or unity of God against what they see as a threat which would err on the side of over-emphasizing the three divine persons.

In the chapters that follow, I will take up the task of examining both biblical texts and theological arguments which have been used in support of ESS. In doing so, I will return to many of the issues raised in this chapter by Giles, Goligher, and Trueman. Although important to this discussion, an examination of the validity of seeing eternal submission as compatible with Nicene Trinitarianism is outside of the limitations of this study. In this paper I will interact with the historical sources only to a very small degree within the examination of biblical texts and theological arguments, and particularly within a discussion of the history of interpretation of 1 Corinthians 15.

Chapter 3

A Biblical Examination of Eternal Submission

Is THE IDEA THAT the Son is eternally submissive to the Father in their immanent relationship a biblical concept? In other words, does the text of Scripture give any indication as to whether or not, apart from this created universe, Jesus submits to his Father? This chapter will examine six different biblical passages, showing that each demonstrate the eternal submission of the Son to the Father in different ways. The argumentation here will be both exegetical and theological, taking into consideration the context of each passage and the argumentation of the author.

John's Presentation of the Eternally Submissive Son

The Gospel of John presents Jesus as both intimately united with God the Father, and yet uncompromisingly distinct from his Father.[1] This is true of the Son in both his eternal life and his incarnate life. In John 1:1, Jesus can be seen being both *with* God (that is, in relationship with the Father), and equal to God. In the next

---

1. Ware, "Equal in Essence," 20.

A Biblical Examination of Eternal Submission

several verses, John alternates from seeing Jesus in his relationship with God the Father (v. 2) back to viewing him as the creator God (v. 3), possessor of life (v. 4), and source of light (vv. 4–5). These initial verses set the pattern for John's Gospel in that the author will alternate between viewing Jesus as fully equal with God and viewing him as the Son of God in relationship with his Father.[2]

John makes an important statement early in the book that speaks about how human beings should view Jesus' relationship to the Father. In John 1:18, John writes, "No man has seen God at any time; the only begotten God, who is in the bosom of the Father, He has explained Him."[3] God has never been seen by human eyes, so our understanding of him must come as he reveals himself to us. We cannot on our own approach him because of sin that resides within us and separates us from him. Later in John, Jesus reveals that God is spirit (John 4:24) in contrast to the physical and earthly nature of human beings. Humanity, therefore, has only a limited knowledge of God, not being able to see or understand him on our own.[4]

The only begotten God, God the Son, reveals the triune God to us. He is in the bosom of the Father, enjoying unique intimacy with him as Son. "The phrase 'in closest relationship' (εἰς τὸν κόλπον) refers to the unmatched intimacy of Jesus' relationship with the Father . . . which enabled him to reveal the Father in an unprecedented way."[5] That intimate, intra-Trinitarian relationship is made known to us through the human life of the man Christ Jesus and the way he interacts with his Father. Jesus reveals the triune God both in his identification with God as partaking in the same divine nature, and in his relational distinction from the Father as the one who was sent, who obeys his Father's will, etc. Köstenberger agrees when he writes:

2. Köstenberger and Swain, *Father, Son*, 47–48.

3. All biblical references are quoted from the New American Standard Bible unless otherwise noted.

4. Köstenberger, *John*, 49. This commentary was recently pulled as a result of inadequate citations. See Köstenberger, "Letter from Dr. Köstenberger."

5. Köstenberger, *John*, 49.

Eternal Submission

John here does not use the more common term for "to make known," γνωρίζω (*gnōrizō* [15:15; 17:26]), but the rare expression ἐξηγέομαι (*exēgeomai*; found only here in this Gospel). In its Lukan occurrences (Luke 24:35; Acts 10:8; 15:12, 14; 21:19), the term regularly means "to give a full account" in the sense of "telling the whole story," the probable meaning here also . . . As he concludes his introduction, John therefore makes the important point that the entire Gospel to follow should be read as an account of Jesus "telling the whole story" of God the Father.[6]

This "telling the whole story of God the Father" refers not only to the whole story as it relates to the economy of salvation, but also the life of God eternally, since John's point is that Jesus makes the unknown known and the invisible visible. Jesus also makes the immanent and unknowable life of God known to mankind, both as it relates to unity of God and the relationships between the persons. There are limits to this revelation, however. We cannot know *everything* about God's immanent life from viewing the life of Jesus. The life of God in himself is too vast, deep, and wide for human beings to ever understand in its entirety. Yet we are able to understand what we see displayed in the life of Christ as a true and real reflection of what the eternal life of God is like.[7] "The evangelist here emphasizes the closeness of relationship between Jesus and the Father as the grounds of the 'full account' (*exēgēsato*) borne by Jesus of the Father (1:18)."[8]

While we surely cannot understand *everything* about God's life *ad intra*, what we see in the relationship between the human Jesus and God the Father must reflect *something* about the eternal reality. Furthermore, if we say Jesus only submits to his Father in his humanity and not in their intra-Trinitarian relations, we have to qualify John 1:18, arguing that Jesus gives a "full account" of who God the Father is in reference to his unity with the Father, but

---

6. Köstenberger, *John*, 50.
7. Thompson, "Trinity and Revelation," 241.
8. Köstenberger and Swain, *Father, Son*, 50.

A Biblical Examination of Eternal Submission

not a "full account" in terms of their relations, since his incarnate submission is not ultimately reflective of eternal realities.

Having made these initial comments, we will now focus in on the eternal submission of the Son from John 6:38. There Jesus says, "For I have come down from heaven, not to do My own will, but the will of Him who sent Me." There are several arguments here. The first is that the very terms "Father" and "Son" imply not only a relationship of origin, but also a filial relationship of authority and obedience. It would be a mistake to read *everything* about the father/son human relationship back into the Trinity,[9] but at the same time the words were chosen by the biblical authors who were inspired by the Holy Spirit to reflect *something* of the relationship between the two divine persons beyond the idea of origin alone.[10] Köstenberger and Swain show that the terms father and son bring out both ideas of *source* and *authority*:

> What [Marianne Meye] Thompson's work on the father-son relationship in the OT suggests is that there exists a biblical model for conceiving a relationship at once characterized by *equality* and *obedience*, the relationship that exists between a father and a son. In biblical anthropology, a son is at once "like" his father as his "image" (Gen. 5:3) and "heir"; but a son is also called to submit to his father's will.[11]

Second, because the Father sends the Son from heaven, the Father possesses authority and the Son demonstrates submission to that authority.[12] In referring to himself as the one sent, Jesus reveals the ordered relational positions of both the Father who has author-

---

9. For example, human sons are begotten by human fathers in a way that is not parallel to God the Father's begetting of the eternal Son.

10. Grudem argues extensively on this point. Grudem, "Biblical Evidence," 227–32.

11. Köstenberger and Swain, *Father, Son,* 119.

12. So Ware, *Father, Son,* 47–48. Here the sending of the Son is an act that is carried out in the temporal world, but has its foundations and planning in eternity. In that regard the temporal manifestation of this sending takes place in the incarnation, but there are also eternal facets of the Father's sending of the Son to consider.

ity to send and the Son who willingly obeys. Grudem says, "The Father *sending* the Son into the world implies an authority that the Father had prior to the Son's humbling himself and becoming a man. This is because to have the authority to send someone means to have a *greater authority* than the one who is sent."[13]

Many object to reading eternal authority and submission into the act of the Father sending the Son. Giles argues in this instance that Jesus, as coequal God with the Father in essence and relation, is the same in authority as the one who sends him:

> It is always tempting to interpret the Scriptures on the basis of human experience, but good exegesis should begin by seeking to discover what the biblical author himself had in mind when he wrote. A more plausible interpretation of this sending language is that it reflects the Jewish *Shaliach* concept. In Judaism the one sent (the *Shaliach*) has the same authority as the one who sends him: he is as the sender himself.[14]

Further, Giles writes,

> This means that the sending terminology in John is best understood as underscoring the unity between the Father and the Son in their work (5:17–18; 10:29–30), and as explaining how the words of the Son are the words of the Father (3:34; 12:50; 14:10–11). The human language of sending distinguishes the persons—the Father is the one who sends, the Son the one who is sent—but the emphasis falls on the authority of the Son as expressing the authority of the Father.[15]

Is John employing Second Temple Jewish thought as he uses the terminology of "sending" to talk about the relationship between Father and Son as Christ comes into the world? A brief examination of John's usage of the term "send" (Greek, πεμπω) renders this judgment unlikely. John uses this term thirty-two times throughout his Gospel, more than any other Gospel writer. Twenty-four of

---

13. Grudem, "Biblical Evidence," 244.
14. Giles, *Jesus and Father*, 119.
15. Giles, *Jesus and Father*, 120.

A Biblical Examination of Eternal Submission

those occurrences refer to the Father's sending of the Son into the world. The other eight occurrences are helpful in evaluating Giles' claim.[16]

In John 1:22, Jewish priests and Levites have come to John the Baptist from Jerusalem asking him to give an answer about who he is. They ask John, "Who are you, so that we may give an answer to those who sent us?" If John is using πεμπω according to the Jewish *Shaliach* concept, why are these priests and Levites adamant that they should not return to those who sent them without an answer about John's identity? John 1:24 makes clear that the ones who had sent the priests and Levites were the Pharisees. In this verse, then, the party that is sent (priests and Levites) is clearly subordinate to the party that sends them (Pharisees).

John 1:33 also depicts a distinction in rank between the one sent and the sender. Here, John the Baptist speaks of himself as the one sent, and the one who sent him to baptize (i.e., God, cf. John 1:6) gives instructions which John obeys. There can be no arguing that John occupies a subordinate role to God here. John 13:16 likewise shows the correspondence between the messenger and the one who sent him likened to the servant being subordinate to his master. Again, this does not depict well the idea of the one sent occupying an equal position with the sender, as in rabbinic thought.

John 13:20 and 20:21 refer to Jesus' sending of his followers into the world, or their commission. It might be argued that the church occupies the same position that Jesus does in this present age, and so the *Shaliach* concept might be in view. However, this would counter later NT teaching on the position of Christ as the head and authority over the church (Eph 1:22, Col 1:18). It is better to see Jesus in a position of authority over his followers as he sends them on mission into the world. Interestingly, Jesus says in John

---

16. Christopher Cowen says here, "A comparison to others who were "sent"—in which John uses the same terminology—reveals their obvious subordination to their sender(s): John the Baptist, who was sent by God (John 1:6, 33); the priests and Levites who were sent by the Jews/Pharisees to question John (1:19, 22, 24); and the officers who were sent by the chief priests and Pharisees to arrest Jesus (7:32; cf. 7:45). So, it seems only natural to see Jesus' relationship to his sender in the same way." Cowen, "Father and Son," 49–50.

20:21, "As the Father has sent Me, I also send you." A comparison is made between the sending of the Son from eternity in heaven to earth, and the sending of Jesus' disciples into the world. If the Father and the Son are viewed as having equal parts in the sending of the Son, what is the comparison to Jesus and his followers? One would have to argue that both Jesus and his followers are equal in authority. Yet as has just been pointed out above, this does not correlate well with the witness of the NT.

Finally, in John 14:25, 15:26, and 16:7 the Holy Spirit is said to be sent from the Father (14:26) and the Son (15:26, 16:7). While the Spirit occupies the same divine nature, it is clear that both God the Father and Jesus are seen as having authority to send the Holy Spirit on his mission related to Jesus' disciples. "The Father is never sent; he is sender of both the Son and the Spirit. The Spirit is never sender; he is sent by both the Father and the Son. Only Jesus is both sent one and sender; sent by the Father, he sends both the Spirit and the disciples."[17] In these instances, the Holy Spirit demonstrates divine submission to the Father and Son as they respectively send him on his mission into the world.

These eight occurrences inform us as readers of John's Gospel that his use of the term πεμπω, apart from a discussion of intra-Trinitarian relationships, regularly follows a pattern where the sender possesses authority over the one who is sent. Certainly, John could be using πεμπω in a different way when referring to the sending of the Son by the Father (and of the Spirit by the Father and Son), but it is much more likely that John uses πεμπω consistently where the sender is authoritative and the one sent submits and obeys. Since God the Father sent Jesus the Son from eternity into temporality, an eternal order of authority and submission between Father and Son is in view.

Third, Jesus is demonstrating in his earthly obedience to the Father his eternal obedience. We may ask the question, why did Jesus come down from heaven? What was his purpose? The answer given in the text is not to do his own will, but the will of the Father. The words, "For I have come down from heaven (ὅτι καταβέβηκα

---

17. Köstenberger, *John*, 442.

A Biblical Examination of Eternal Submission

ἀπὸ τοῦ οὐρανοῦ)," indicate that this is the purpose of the Son in his coming. This purpose must have been determined by the Son *prior to* his incarnation while he was still in heaven, which then led to or caused his coming down. Jesus came down from heaven for the purpose of doing his Father's will, and that intention was determined in eternity.

Notice also that the Son freely chose to do his Father's will from eternity. Jesus does not present any divine coercion on the part of his Father within their immanent relationship.[18] Instead, the verb "I have come down" (καταβέβηκα) presents the Son's voluntary decision to execute the will of his Father.[19] Jesus as the divine Son of God knows that the Father has authority to send him into the world, and yet at the same time he presents his coming as a willful decision made in eternity to enact his Father's will on the earth.[20] This reveals that in the mind of the incarnate Son there is no contradiction between saying that the Father had authority to send the Son, and at the same time that the Son on some level chose to obey that authority.

The fourth argument concerns Jesus' future execution of the will of the Father. Jesus reveals the Father's will in verse 39: "And this is the will of Him who sent Me, that of all that He has given Me I lose nothing, but raise it up on the last day." This shows that Jesus, in submitting to and obeying the Father's will, continues to do his Father's will *after* his death and resurrection. The "last day" of this verse has a clear eschatological connection. Jesus' obedience and submission to the Father continues all the way down to the eschatological end, but opponents of ESS want to argue that the Son

---

18. It should be reiterated here that the distinctions being addressed between Father and Son here are not essential distinctions but personal distinctions. The unity between Father and Son is demonstrated in that they both work to accomplish the one goal of losing no one but raising them on the last day (John 6:39). Both Father and Son possess full deity. What is being discussed here is their relational distinctions.

19. Kevin Giles argues this same point when addressing John 6:38–39. Giles, *Jesus and Father*, 121–22.

20. For a fuller discussion of the one divine will as it relates to discussion of the wills of the Father and Son, see chapter 5 below.

ceases to be obedient in the "form of a servant" at his resurrection and ascension.[21] John 6:38 firmly refutes this misconception. The Son does not cease to be obedient and submissive at the resurrection but continues to do his Father's will in his glorified condition, as we are told here, until the last day.

The Gospel of John presents Jesus as both equal to the Father and one with him, sent by him, and voluntarily submissive to his Father's will. We have seen the Father's authority and the Son's submission demonstrated in the terms "Father" and "Son," in the sending of the Son by the Father, in the obedience of the Son to the Father, and in the determination of the Son to accomplish his Father's will on the last day. There is a beautiful complexity in John's presentation of Jesus: Jesus is God in full, and yet Jesus submits to God. Bruce Ware summarizes this powerfully in saying, "One might think that if he is God, then he wouldn't be under anyone's authority, or if he is a Son, then he couldn't be fully divine. But divine he is, and a Son he is. As God the Son, he submits to God his Father."[22]

Jesus the Eternally-Appointed Messianic Son and High Priest

In Hebrews 5:5–6, Christ is spoken of as not taking to himself a high priesthood, but receiving it from God the Father during his humanity. Letham argues that the divine decision to appoint Christ as high priest occurred in eternity:

> His appointment to the work of high priest is prior to the work itself and so prior to his incarnation. The idea is that the Son "did not exalt himself." He did not seek this

---

21. Giles, *Trinity & Subordinationism*, 30–31, 116. Giles writes, "The lowly, subordinated, suffering Christ is exalted to reign forever as the Lord. In his exaltation he leaves behind all the limitations that his taking flesh involved. Rather than his continuing existence as God and man making him a little less than equal God, his glorified state makes his humanity God-like." Giles, *Jesus and Father*, 107. See also Giles, "Son of God," 15, 18.

22. Ware, *Father, Son*, 74.

A Biblical Examination of Eternal Submission

task for his own advantage. He did not claim the office. He was appointed to it, and his appointment was made by the Father.[23]

This divine appointment was made in eternity, signifying the eternal nature of the Son's submissive disposition. Within this appointment we see God the Father possessing authority to bestow the position of high priest on the Son, and the Son willingly receiving that position.

A survey of Hebrews 4:14–5:10 shows this is the case. From 4:14 onward, the focus shifts from the kingship of Jesus to his priesthood, both in terms of priestly characteristics and priestly actions. Hebrews 4:14–5:10 displays his qualifications as priest, culminating in obedience to God (Heb 5:8). In Hebrews 4:14–16 Jesus' humanity and empathy are in view. He is able to sympathize with our weaknesses, having been tempted as we have but remaining pure (Heb 4:15). Hebrews 5:1–5 deals with the qualifications of a high priest: he is appointed on behalf of men to offer sacrifices and gifts (v. 1); he can deal gently with the weak since he is also weak; he offers sacrifices for his own sins as well as the people's; and he is called by God. In a loose chiastic structure, Hebrews 5:5–10 shows how Christ meets the qualifications for high priest in that he was called by God (vv. 5–6), he offered prayers and supplications (v. 7, cf. gifts and sacrifices in v. 1), he suffered [in weakness] (v. 8, c.f. v. 2–3), and he became the source of eternal salvation (v. 9, c.f. v. 3).[24]

Verses 5 and 6 show the qualifications of Christ for priesthood. The first phrase of verse 5 reveals that "Christ did not glorify Himself so as to become a high priest." This is set in comparison to what is said in verse 4 of the Levitical priests: "And no one takes the honor to himself, but receives it when he is called by God, even as Aaron was." In other words, just as the Levitical priests were called by God to service, so Christ was appointed by God as a high priest. The *execution* of this appointment takes place during Christ's humanity. He is a human high priest; if he were not,

23. Letham, *Holy Trinity*, 404.

24. Allen sees a strict chiastic structure in the qualifications. Allen, *Hebrews*, 313–14.

he would not be able to "sympathize with our weaknesses," (Heb 4:15). His high priesthood is a human office, although this high priest is seated in heaven.

Yet the *planning* of Christ's appointment as high priest occurred within the mind of God prior to the incarnation in eternity. The reason for this is that the author quotes OT texts, which would have been written prior to the incarnation, as speaking ultimately of Jesus. "So also Christ did not glorify Himself so as to become a high priest, but He who said to Him, 'You are My Son, today I have begotten You'; just as He says also in another passage, 'You are a priest forever according to the order of Melchizedek,'" (Heb 5:5-6). The author of Hebrews applies Psalm 2:7 and 110:4 to Christ, and so his appointment as high priest must have been conceived in the divine council of the Godhead well before the incarnation, since these OT texts speak of the Father calling the Son to sonship and priesthood at a time when the eternal Son of God was not yet the incarnate Son of God.

In reading that God the Father spoke to the Son and said, "You are My Son, today I have begotten You," the question rises as to when the execution of this proclamation occurred. The most satisfying answer is to locate this proclamation temporally at Jesus' resurrection and exaltation.[25] A short study of the use of Psalm 2:7 in the NT provides support for this interpretation.

The quotation is used three times in the NT: once by Luke in Acts 13:33, and twice by the author of Hebrews (1:5; 5:5). In Acts 13:33, Paul is presenting the gospel to the Jews at Antioch in Pisidia (Asia Minor) and arguing that Jesus fulfilled the OT promises. In verses 30-37 the resurrection of Jesus is the key proof that the promises made to the OT saints are now being realized. In verses 32-33 Paul says, "And we preach to you the good news of the promise made to the fathers, that God has fulfilled this promise to our children in that He raised up Jesus, as it is also written

---

25. I reiterate here that the *determination* that Christ would be a high priest occurred in eternity, as demonstrated by the fact that it was predicted during the time of David in the composition of Psalms 2 and 110. Yet the *execution* of that plan temporally occurred when Christ was declared to be the Son of God at his resurrection.

A Biblical Examination of Eternal Submission

in the second Psalm, 'You are My Son; today I have begotten You.'" Here, Psalm 2:7 is quoted to show that the resurrection is proof of Jesus' appointment as divine Son. Verses 34–37 go on to argue from two other OT passages that Jesus is the greater David who did not see decay, further connecting Psalm 2:7 with Jesus' resurrection. Acts 13:33, then, connects Psalm 2:7 with Jesus' resurrection and exaltation.

In Hebrews 1:5, the author has just argued for the exaltation of the risen Christ. "When He had made purification of sins, He sat down at the right hand of the Majesty on high; having become as much better than the angels, as He has inherited a more excellent name than they," (Heb 1:3–4). Jesus has been exalted to the right hand of God, and so has received higher glory than any angelic being. It is in this context that we have verse 5: "For to which of the angels did He ever say, 'You are My Son, Today I have begotten You'? And again, 'I will be a Father to Him and He shall be a Son to Me'?" Hebrews 1:5 situates Psalm 2:7's proclamation at the exaltation of Christ to the right hand of the Father.

Coming back to Hebrews 5:5, based on the other NT occurrences of Psalm 2:7, it would be most consistent to view God the Father's proclamation declaring Jesus to be the divine Son as taking place after his resurrection and exaltation to the Father's right hand.[26] This means that after the resurrection God the Father declares Jesus to be the messianic Son prophesied by Psalm 2:7.[27] The Father possesses the authority to proclaim the Son to be the anointed ruler. Not only is this proclamation planned in advance of the incarnation, it is enacted after the resurrection, when many

---

26. Interestingly, this would be after Giles believes Jesus' temporary submission to the Father has ended. He says, "In contrast to Grudem, who thinks that there is no significant change in Christ's status after the resurrection, the New Testament makes this event epoch changing. The lowly, subordinated, suffering Christ is exalted to reign forever as the Lord. In his exaltation he leaves behind all the limitations that his taking flesh involved. Rather than his continuing existence as God and man making him a little less than equal God, his glorified state makes his humanity God-like." Giles, *Jesus and Father*, 107.

27. Cf. Romans 1:4, "who was declared the Son of God with power by the resurrection from the dead, according to the Spirit of holiness, Jesus Christ our Lord."

Eternal Submission

who oppose the idea of eternal submission would argue Christ has ceased submitting to his Father, since he is once again exalted to the Father's throne.

The use of Psalm 110:4 in Hebrews 5:6 is even more instructive to the discussion of ESS. In saying that Christ is a priest forever, again the question rises as to when his priesthood began. The fact that this OT text is put in conjunction with Psalm 2:7 argues for a similar conclusion as was drawn there. When Psalm 110:4 is used later in Hebrews, it is in conjunction with the resurrection of Christ. In Hebrews 7, the author twice points out that Jesus' priesthood is legitimized as an enduring, everlasting priesthood because of the resurrection. Verse 16 refers to Jesus' "power of an indestructible life," a reference to his resurrected, glorified existence before quoting Psalm 110:4 in verse 17. Verse 24 likewise gives a commentary on Psalm 110:4 when the author writes, "but Jesus, on the other hand, *because He continues forever*, holds His priesthood permanently," (emphasis mine). Jesus is a priest forever because of the resurrection, when God the Father installs the eternal Son as the everlasting priest.

Thus, we see that Jesus' appointment by God to the office of messianic ruler and high priest should be located after his resurrection and exaltation to the right hand of the Father. Therefore, after the resurrection, God the Father possesses the authority to declare Jesus messianic ruler and great high priest, and Jesus accepts that position. This demonstrates authority and submission between Father and Son in their present intra-Trinitarian relationship.[28]

I have argued above that the temporal appointment of Christ to the office of messianic Son and great high priest is most properly located at the exaltation of Christ. The planning of this

---

28. It could be argued that the present state of Christ's existence is a continuation of the incarnation. Yet Christ's ascension to the right hand of the Father is spoken of throughout the NT as an ascension into heaven, where he had previously been. Christ speaks of recovering the glory he previously had with the Father in John 17:5. There is, then, a sense of consistency between Christ's pre-incarnate position with the Father and his post-ascension exaltation. Therefore, we should not limit this scene as pertaining to the economic Trinity alone, but indicative of their immanent relationship.

appointment occurred in advance of the incarnation as demonstrated by the citation of OT texts. The fact that the author to the Hebrews cites OT texts to illustrate this shows that this was not whimsical but already premeditated in the mind of God before the incarnation of the Son back during the time when David wrote, and even further back to the time of the Patriarchs when Melchizedek served as a type of the greater king-priest to come. As the OT texts were penned, God the Father had already planned to appoint the eternal Son to messianic sonship and high priesthood at his right hand in heaven.

Prior to the incarnation, then, Hebrews 5:5–6 portrays the Father as possessing authority over the Son, and the Son willingly accepting the appointment given to him by the Father. It could be argued that perhaps this appointment was planned by both Father and Son in eternity, and then enacted by the Father temporally. Yet the biblical texts examined above give no support to this idea. Rather, they present God the Father as authoritative to appoint the Son to his position, and the Son as receptive of the appointment. If the relationship between Father and Son as it relates to this appointment is altogether different in the economy of salvation than in eternity, then there are two different trinities in view, one which we can know, and the other which is unknowable to us. If there is one Trinity, the relationship between the two persons in the economy is reflective and consistent with the relationship between the two in eternity.

The Eternally Submissive Mindset of the Son

Philippians 2:5–11 shows a determination by the Son in eternity. Christ Jesus, "although He existed in the form of God, did not *regard* equality with God a thing to be grasped, but emptied Himself, taking the form of a bond-servant, and being made in the likeness of men," (Phil 2:6–7). The key term for our discussion is "regard," (ἡγησατο) and shows us something of the thought process of the eternal Son in the immanent Trinity. Letham says here, "His decision to [empty himself] was made prior to his doing it. His determination not to exploit his true and real status for his own advantage was made in eternity. His self-emptying on earth flowed from his refusal to pursue self-interest in eternity. His human obedience reflects his divine submission."[29] Philippians 2:6–7 therefore gives a glimpse into the eternal submission of the Son.[30]

Tracing Paul's argument through Philippians 2 sets the stage for our discussion. In verses 1–4 Paul encourages his readers to make his joy complete by "being of the same mind, maintaining the same love, united in spirit, intent on one purpose" (Phil 2:2). This focus on unity is underlined in verses 3–4 with two contrasts that illustrate his point. First, in verse 3 he urges readers to do nothing from "selfishness or empty conceit," but to consider others more important than themselves with "humility of mind." Second, in verse 4, being of the same mind involves not looking out only for personal interests, but instead being concerned for the interests of others. Lynn Cohick says on verse 4, "The verse aims to de-center the self, not to set up guidelines that establish when enough is enough and when you can focus on yourself."[31] Thus, verses 5–11 are set up to be an illustration of how believers can have humility of mind and concern for the interests of others.

In verses 5–11, this "humility of mind" is equated with the attitude of Christ Jesus (v. 5), and believers are commanded to have his attitude in their relationships with one another. If Jesus, who eternally existed with God in "the form of God" (v. 6), humbled himself to take on humanity (v. 7) and willingly die (v. 8), believers in Christ ought to exhibit the same humility. Christ's humility in verses 5–8 leads to his exaltation in verses 9–11, and the implication is perhaps that humility in this lifetime will lead to reward and exaltation in the next.

In verses 5–11, there appears to be a progression from Christ's preincarnate glory to his resurrected glory; in other words, a chronological sequence exists in Paul's argument here. Verse 6 displays his preincarnate life with the Father. He "existed in the

---

29. Letham, *Holy Trinity*, 403.
30. Letham, "Does the Son?," 14.
31. Cohick, *Philippians*, 95.

form of God," (ἐν μορφῇ θεοῦ ὑπάρχων), which should be read in context with the next phrase, "equality with God."[32] The form of God and equality with God both speak of Christ's preexistence. Christ "did not regard equality with God a thing to be grasped" (οὐχ ἁρπαγμὸν ἡγήσατο τὸ εἶναι ἴσα θεῷ), but emptied himself by taking on humanity. This is the key phrase in this passage for the ESS debate, and the key verb is ἡγήσατο, "think, regard, consider."

The verb shows the mental process of the eternal Son *before* his incarnation. The first phrase of verse 6 shows the Son's sharing of full deity. The second phrase indicates that, at the same time, in eternity apart from the created world, the Son did not mentally think about his divine equality with the Father as something to be used for his own advantage but emptied himself through the incarnation. The use of the accusative ἁρπαγμὸν has been heavily debated, but could render the meaning that Christ, in full possession of divine nature, did not consider using this for his own benefit, and so go against the will of his Father (cf. John 6:39). Richard Melick, Jr. says here:

> Since he already possessed "equality with God," Jesus had nothing to grasp. He was able to release the appearance of deity... The passage may mean, therefore, that Christ did not think of his equality as "something to use for his own advantage."[33]

Philippians 2:6, then, demonstrates the eternal Son's refusal to use his own deity selfishly, and instead his willingly taking humanity to himself for the good of others. It presents Christ's mental thought process as one where the Son of God, fully God himself, freely and voluntarily emptied himself through becoming incarnate. Letham agrees:

> The Son's self-emptying, his seeking the interests of the others in his incarnate ministry, is not alien to who God

---

32. Cohick, *Philippians*, 112. Cohick writes, "Indeed, *morphē* is an elastic term that gains nuance from its context. In our case, that context is the phrase 'equality with God.'" Cohick, *Philippians*, 112.

33. Melick, Jr., *Philippians, Colossians*, 103.

is. This is what God is like. The Son freely chose to become man. He did not regard his equality with God as something to be exploited. His actions in the gospels mirrored his determination in eternity; they were far from incongruous.[34]

The authority of the Father over the Son is demonstrated in several ways in this passage. First, it is seen in the preincarnate determination of the Son to empty himself through the taking of humanity. Though Paul in Philippians does not tell us that the Son is obeying his Father as that is not his emphasis, we know from corresponding NT texts that the Father sent the Son into the world. This shows within the intra-Trinitarian relationship both the cooperative working of the persons in unity (the Father sending the Son and the Son obeying), as well as the distinctive, submissive disposition of the Son to freely determine to humble himself.

The authority of the Father is also demonstrated in the Son's being obedient to death, even death on a cross (v. 8). The Son, as we saw above, never ceases to be fully God. The intra-Trinitarian relationship between Father and Son does not change at the incarnation; as they eternally have been, they forever continuously are and will be. To say that the Son only obeys the Father in terms of his humanity in Philippians 2:8 creates a dangerous disjoint in terms of the person of Christ.[35] The divine and human natures of Jesus are united together perfectly in the person of the Son. It follows, then, that obedience demonstrated in the incarnation flows out of eternal submission and obedience.[36]

---

34. Letham, "Reply to Kevin Giles," 344.

35. This disjoint, if left unchecked, could be left to wander toward Nestorianism, effectively creating an immanent Son and an economic Son.

36. This is the conclusion of Wallace in his study of Philippians 2. He says, "Although Christ was truly God (μορφῇ θεοῦ), two things resulted: (1) he did not attempt to 'outrank' the Father, as it were (c.f. John 14:28 for a similar thought: 'The Father is greater than I am'); (2) instead, he submitted himself to the Father's will, even to the point of death on a cross. It was thus not Christ's deity that compelled his incarnation and passion, but his obedience." Wallace, *Greek Grammar*, 635.

A Biblical Examination of Eternal Submission

Finally, God the Father's exaltation of Christ to the highest position, with the highest name, shows the Father's primacy in power in Paul's thinking and the Son's submission to that power. The Son becomes the highest authority in this created universe after his death and resurrection. Yet he is raised to that position by God the Father. The one who exalts Jesus and bestows on him the name above all names by necessary implication possesses authority over the Son in some way. This is made explicit by the phrase "to the glory of God the Father" (v. 11).[37] Jesus' exaltation is ultimately for the Father's glory and not his own, driving home Paul's point of having an attitude of humility that looks out for the interests of others. Throughout his preincarnate, incarnate, and glorified existence, the Son looks out for the interests of God the Father and of humanity over and above his own interests.

This passage demonstrates, theologically, the submission of the Son to the Father from before the incarnation, throughout his humanity, after his resurrection, and into the eschatological future when every knee will bow and every tongue will confess that Jesus Christ is Lord to the glory of God the Father (Phil 2:9–11).

Christ's Eschatological Deliverance of the Kingdom to His Father

First Corinthians 15:24–28 without a doubt shows the subjection of Christ to God the Father in the economy of salvation, but does this have implications for the unending future? In these verses, the Son hands the kingdom over to the Father at the eschatological end and is himself subjected to God the Father just as he subjected

---

37. This is against Cohick's view that this quotation "points to their one essence." She says, "This final phrase is not making gradations of honor between Father and Son; instead it insists that Son and Father are of the same essence—both God." Cohick, *Philippians*, 124. I find this argument unconvincing in that while Christ's exaltation ultimately honors God the Father, the Father's glory is viewed as the *telos* of the exaltation of the Son. "Thus this final sentence begins with God's exalting Christ by bestowing on him *the name* and concludes on the same theological note, that all of this is to God the Father's own *glory*." Fee, *Philippians*, 101.

Eternal Submission

all things to the Son (v. 28). At the end of human history and the recreation of the heavens and the earth, then, we see the authority of the Father and the submission of the Son displayed into the endless future ages.

It will be helpful to begin with a survey of 1 Corinthians 15:20–28, presenting the case for ESS at critical points. This passage shows the apostle Paul discussing the importance of the resurrection. In verse 20, Christ is the "first fruits" of those who had "fallen asleep," meaning his resurrection was just the beginning of further future human resurrections. In verses 21–22 a connection is made between Adam and Christ, with their actions having sweeping effects on humanity: Adam's sin brought death to the human race; Christ's death brings life to all who believe; and so resurrection from death. Verses 23–24 discuss the order of resurrection events. First Christ is resurrected. Next, when he comes, those who are his at his coming are raised to life again. "Then," Paul says, "comes the end, when He delivers up the kingdom to the God and Father, when He has abolished all rule and all authority and power" (1 Cor 15:24). This verse has implications for the ESS debate in that the resurrected Christ hands his kingdom over to the Father at the eschatological end.[38] Paul will expound on this in verses 27–28.

Verses 25–26 speak of Christ reigning until all his enemies have been subjected to him, the last enemy being death. The next verse says, "For He has put all things in subjection under His feet. But when He says, 'All things are put in subjection,' it is evident that He is excepted who put all things in subjection to Him," (1 Cor 15:27). Both the context surrounding this verse and the context of Psalm 110:1, from which Paul is drawing, make clear that this is not the Son subjecting all things to himself, but the Father subjecting all things to the Son, with the exception of the Father himself. The Father is not subjected to the Son in this passage.[39]

---

38. Ware, *Father, Son*, 84. Ware says here, "There is no question that this passage indicates the eternal future submission of the Son to the Father, in keeping with his submission to the Father both in the incarnation and in eternity past." Ware, *Father, Son*, 84.

39. Giles argues along the lines of Pannenberg in advocating for a mutual submission between Father and Son here. Giles, *Jesus and Father*, 114–15.

A Biblical Examination of Eternal Submission

Proponents of ESS see an order of authority here that pertains to the future rule of Christ. The Father is the possessor of all who places all things in subjection under his Son's feet, who is in turn subject to the Father.

Finally, in verse 28 Paul says, "And when all things are subjected to Him, then the Son Himself also will be subjected to the one who subjected all things to Him, that God may be all in all." At the end, when death and all other enemies have finally been subjected to Christ, Christ himself will be subjected to "the one who subjected all things to him," namely, God the Father. The subjection of the Son to the Father appears to be a reality that continues into the endless ages of the future.

Opponents of ESS argue against authority and submission in this passage. Giles' argument at this point is as follows:

> What Paul thus seems to be suggesting is that the rule God the Father gave to God the Son at the resurrection is freely handed back to the Father by the Son at the end. Rather than speaking of fixed roles, or of the eternal subordination of the Son, this text indicates a changing of roles in differing epochs.[40]

Giles' interpretation does not account well for the grammatical construction of "the Son Himself also will be subjected to the One who subjected all things to Him," ([καὶ] αὐτὸς ὁ υἱὸς ὑποταγήσεται τῷ ὑποτάξαντι αὐτῷ τὰ πάντα) in verse 28. The text is emphatic that it is the Son *himself* who is subjected to the same God, God the Father, who subjected all things to him. Leon Morris comments here, "Paul hammers home his point by using the same verb six times in two verses. The climax of this process of 'putting under' comes when the Son (the one occurrence of this designation of Jesus in Paul) is 'put under' the Father."[41] Since this is the last action that precedes the eternal state, the Son's subjection to the Father has implications for the everlasting future because of the final phrase "that God may be all in all." In other words, God is all in all because

---

40. Giles, "Doctrine of Trinity," 284.
41. Morris, *1 Corinthians*, 213.

all things are subject to Christ the Son who is himself voluntarily subject to his Father in their immanent and eternal relationship. The temporal, material reality fully matches the eternal reality.

To argue that 1 Corinthians 15:24–28 shows "a changing of roles in differing epochs" as Giles does implies that there are occasions when God the Father takes a submissive role and the Son an authoritative one. The Father, however, is *never* said to be subjected to the Son in the Scriptures. He is always the authoritarian in their relationship.

D. Glenn Butner, Jr. has recently argued against seeing the eternal submission of the Son in this passage.[42] Admirably, he attempts to understand 1 Corinthians 15:24–28 in light of the entire context of 1 Corinthians 15. In so doing, he places much emphasis on Paul's description of Christ as the second Adam. Butner, Jr. sees reference to Psalm 110:1 and Psalm 8:6 in 1 Corinthians 15:27 as focusing on the human office of Christ as second Adam and human viceregent.[43] Rather than seeing Christ submitting to the Father at the eschatological end, Butner, Jr. sees the human reign of Christ terminating and being replaced by "God's direct rule."[44] "Christ will reign as second Adam, the human viceregent with God. Then, at some point, this human reign as second Adam will end, 'so that God may be all in all' (15:28b)."[45] Butner, Jr. concludes, "What Paul has in mind in verse 28 has nothing to do with the eternal relation between Father and Son, and everything to do with Christ's human status as second Adam, a status that Paul reveals will one day be supplanted by the even greater grace of God's direct rule."[46]

---

42. Butner, Jr., *The Son*, 162–72.

43. Butner, Jr., *The Son*, 170. Jesus' use of Ps 110:1 in Matt 22:41–46 points to the fact that the Psalm is meant to point out more than the human office of the Messiah here. That is Jesus' point in asking "If David then calls Him 'Lord,' how is He his son?" The answer is meant to point out the dual natures of Christ: he is fully man, but also fully God. He is David's son (humanity), but also David's Lord (deity).

44. Butner, Jr., *The Son*, 171.

45. Butner, Jr., *The Son*, 170.

46. Butner, Jr., *The Son*, 170–71.

A Biblical Examination of Eternal Submission

This assertion, however, has at least two major problems. First, what distinguishes the reign of the risen Christ as second Adam from his reign after the time described in 1 Corinthians 15:28? Butner, Jr.'s description of the human reign of Christ ending creates a sharp distinction between the humanity and deity of Christ. He says, "Paul appears to teach of Christ's reign as second Adam for a time, much akin to the millennial reign in Revelation, but this time will end and there will be a final consummation in which creation can then be directly subject to God without Adamic mediation."[47] Yet the hypostatic union means Christ continues in his humanity into the unending future. Jesus never sheds his humanity. Beyond 1 Corinthians 15:28, Jesus continues as both God and man perfectly united. There is no end, therefore, to the Adamic mediation of Christ. To say that 1 Corinthians 15:24–28 applies only to the humanity of Christ wrongly dichotomizes the person of Christ. There is no human Christ distinct from a divine Christ; there is only one person. Butner, Jr.'s suggestion that Christ's "Adamic mediation" will be different from "God's direct rule" does not do justice to the person of Christ or the hypostatic union.

Second, saying that "Adamic mediation" will be replaced by "God's direct rule" is unfortunate wording in that it implies the initial reign of Christ during the millennial kingdom is something less than God's direct rule. This cannot be the case, however, because the risen and glorified Christ shares fully the divine nature and as such is not only the image of the invisible God (Col 1:15), but is also the fullness of deity in bodily form (Col 2:9). Christ's earthly reign in Revelation 20 is not some sort of lesser rule of God over humanity, but the absolute rule of the triune God reigning sovereignly over creation in the incarnate person of the enthroned Lord Jesus Christ.

First Corinthians 15: 24–28, therefore, is neither speaking to changing of roles in variant epochs of human history, nor solely to the temporal reign of the human Christ, but has in mind the end of human history in its present form and presents the relational authority structure between Father and Son into the unending future

---

47. Butner, Jr., *The Son*, 171

Eternal Submission

as one where the Father is authoritarian and his Son is submissive. As D. A. Carson says,

> The most natural reading of these verses is that the Son, the exalted God-man, remains, after the consummation, eternally subject to his Father, no longer the exclusive mediator of the Father's sovereignty—though the final clause, "so that God [not the 'Father'] may be all in all," lays the emphasis on (the Trinitarian) God. If being "made subject to" the Father does not entail some kind of intrinsic inferiority (which is at this juncture almost unthinkable), then why should any sort of functional submission among the persons of the Godhead be thought to entail ontological inferiority?[48]

This passage, then, shows that the glorified Christ of the future continues to be submissive to God the Father, and will continue to be submissive into the great unknown beyond human history.

God the Father's Authority Over the Risen, Glorified Christ

Revelation 1:1–2 portrays the Son, after his resurrection and ascension to the Father, still submissive to the Father's authority. At the beginning of the book of Revelation we read:

> The Revelation of Jesus Christ, which God gave Him to show to His bond-servants, the things which must shortly take place; and He sent and communicated it by His angel to His bond-servant John, who bore witness to the word of God and to the testimony of Jesus Christ, even to all that he saw (Rev. 1:1–2).

The book of Revelation begins with the phrase Ἀποκάλυψις Ἰησοῦ Χριστοῦ (the revelation of Jesus Christ). This genitive construction could mean "the revelation *concerning* or *about* Jesus Christ," or the possessive "Jesus Christ's revelation." I favor the latter view in that while the content of Revelation ultimately concerns Jesus

---

48. Carson, "John 5:26," 95.

A Biblical Examination of Eternal Submission

Christ, it is presented more properly as his possession which he entrusts to John by means of an angel.[49] In either case, the very next phrase indicates that this revelation did not originate with the second person of the Trinity, but belonged to God the Father. God had original possession of this revelation and *gave* (ἔδωκεν) it to Jesus.[50] "Syntactically it is God who reveals and whose acts are performed here. God gives the revelation to Christ."[51]

This revelation was given by God the Father to the Son so that he might show (δεῖξαι) it to his slaves, that is, to those who follow him. The infinitive δεῖξαι reveals the purpose of the sovereign God. God's desire in giving the apocalypse to Christ was that he would reveal it to his servants. Jesus the Son, in turn, revealed it by sending his angel to his servant, John. "Jesus did not initiate the book of Revelation on his own, but he was *given* this revelation by the Father and *authorized* by the Father to deliver it to the church."[52]

The Father possesses and gives his revelation to the Son, and it becomes *his* [the Son's] message or testimony (v. 2). The Son shows this revelation, by the sending of his angel, to John. The message comes from the top down. The Father originates and gives the message to the Son, showing the primacy of the Father in their post-ascension interactions. The Son does not give the message to the Father. The Son, instead, receives the message and passes it down the chain. In Revelation 1:1, then, there is an order of primacy that demonstrates the authority between the Father and the

---

49. It may well be the case that just as "God's word" is both the word possessed by God and a word concerning God that the revelation of Jesus Christ has the same nuances of meaning here.

50. The dative αὐτῷ in verse 1 should be seen as referring to Jesus Christ because it is the best and most natural candidate. Grant Osborne writes, "Jesus is the obvious antecedent of αὐτῷ, and the idea of Jesus' communicating God's message parallels the Gospel of John . . . where it is part of the chain of revelation from God to Jesus to the Holy Spirit to the disciples to the world. Here the chain is from God to Jesus to the angel to John to the churches." Osborne, *Revelation*, 53.

51. De Smidt, Meta-Theology of ὁ Θεός," 187.

52. Grudem, "Biblical Evidence," 247.

Eternal Submission

resurrected and ascended Son. The authority structure in regard to this revelation is as follows:

Character	Relationship to Revelation
Father	Originates revelation and gives revelation to the Son
Son	Receives revelation from the Father and sends it through his angel to John
Angel	Receives revelation from the Son and communicates it to John
John	Receives revelation from the Son as communicated through his angel

Authority Structure in Revelation 1:1

God the Father possesses highest authority in that the message originates with him and he gives it to the Son.[53] Yet the Son's authority is presented as being absolute in that the revelation is spoken of as his possession (notice the parallel in verse 2 between "word of God" and "testimony of Jesus Christ"). This is John's beautiful way of showing that from one perspective (that of divine essence), both persons possess authority when it comes to this revelation, and yet, from another perspective (that of divine relations), God the Father has primacy and the Son derives his authority from the Father.[54]

In verse 2, John bears witness to everything he sees, that is, the word of God and the testimony of Jesus Christ. Rather than being two distinct revelatory messages, the word of God should be equated with the testimony of Jesus Christ in verse 2.[55] We are

---

53. Beale sees an allusion in Rev 1:1 to Dan 2:28–29, 45. The God who sovereignly reveals mysteries to Nebuchadnezzar is also the God who gives the revelation to Jesus, who then gives it to his servants. Beale, "Influence of Daniel," 415.

54. De Smidt, "Meta-Theology of ὁ Θεός," 191–93.

55. De Smidt, "Meta-Theology of ὁ Θεός," 200–1. De Smidt says, "It is possible that the writer applies his usual method to make a general term (τον λόγον τοῦ θεοῦ) more specific by using another phrase (την μαρτυρίαν Ἰησοῦ Χριστοῦ) for more clarity. Rev is therefore the word of God and the witness of Jesus Christ. Through the chain of communication John's witness comes through unfalsified and clear as the Word of God and the witness of Jesus Christ. It does not contain anything new, but summarises once again the divine truth(s)." De Smidt, "Meta-Theology of ὁ Θεός," 200–1.

A Biblical Examination of Eternal Submission

simply looking at the same message from two different perspectives. The revelation is the testimony of Jesus Christ, just as it is *his* revelation (v. 1), and yet at the same time, it is ultimately the word of God the Father who gave it to the Son (v. 1). There is one revelatory message coming from the triune God, yet it comes down from the Father, who gives it to the Son, who sends it by his angel to the apostle John. This again demonstrates a unity in the work of the divine persons to reveal, and at the same time, diversity or distinction in which persons are responsible for communicating that revelation to distinct parties (i.e., God the Father gives it to Christ, Christ shows it to his followers).

Revelation 1:1–2 is a passage that those who reject ESS must explain. If Jesus is only submissive to the Father in terms of his humanity, how should we understand the ordering of authority demonstrated in this passage which takes place *after* the resurrection at a point when many would argue the Son no longer submits to his Father, but in his glorified eternal state possesses coequality with the Father in terms of authority? This passage displays one divine authority when viewed through the lens of the divine *essence*, and yet also displays multiplicity of authority (the Father *gave* the revelation to the Son, and yet the revelation is the possession of the Son) when viewed through the lens of the divine *persons*.[56]

This passage also highlights again the importance of the hypostatic union to the discussion of ESS. If Jesus, as the eternal Son, takes to himself at the incarnation humanity, and that unity of divinity and humanity is an everlasting condition for the Son, at what point would Jesus stop submitting to the Father? Does his divinity overpower his humanity after the resurrection? Even the phrasing of this question betrays Nestorian leanings.[57] Opponents

---

56. At present, I am not aware of any opponents of ESS who hold that Christ continues to submit after his resurrection and ascension in his glorified humanity.

57. Nestorianism is defined by Grudem as "the doctrine that there were two separate persons in Christ, a human person and a divine person, a teaching that is distinct from the biblical view that sees Jesus as one person . . . Nowhere in Scripture do we have an indication of the human and divine natures talking to each other or struggling within Christ, or any such thing. Rather,

of ESS have not offered an adequate answer to explain why Jesus submits to the Father in his humanity *before* the resurrection *but not after* the resurrection and/or ascension.

Revelation 1:1–2 shows, then, the post-resurrection Christ in his ascended, glorified condition continuing to relate to the Father in terms of the Father's authority and the Son's submission. The Father first possesses the revelation that is given to Christ and then becomes Christ's possession to distribute to his servants. This does not take away from the close unity and identification of God and Christ but adds, within divine unity, an element of divine relationality where one person is authoritative and another person is receptive and submissive.

First Corinthians 11:3 Revisited

The last passage I want to examine is 1 Corinthians 11:3. In the debate surrounding the eternal submission of the Son, this has been a much used and often abused verse. Both Grudem and Ware have championed the verse as definitive for their argument.[58] Their contention is that 1 Corinthians 11:3 must refer to the eternal submission of the Son to the Father, since "God is the head of Christ." Ware says,

> In this chapter (1 Corinthians 11) where Paul is about to deal with the importance of women acknowledging the headship of men in the community of faith by wearing head coverings, he prefaces his remarks by describing authority and submission that exist in the eternal Godhead.[59]

For Grudem and Ware, the eternal Trinitarian relations in view in this verse are the basis for male headship and female submission to male headship.

---

we have a consistent picture of a single person acting in wholeness and unity." Grudem, *Systematic Theology*, 554–55.

58. Ware, *Father, Son*, 72–73; Grudem, *Biblical Foundations*, 47.

59. Ware, *Father, Son*, 72.

A Biblical Examination of Eternal Submission

Giles argues to the contrary, saying that the term "head" in this verse does not denote "authority over."[60] He warns against making the connection between God and Christ with man and woman too close. "The human example cannot be used to univocally define the divine relationship. The Father and Son do not relate to one another in exactly the same way as a man and a woman might do, and to suggest so is bad theology."[61] Giles goes on to assert that 1 Corinthians 11:3 does not teach a hierarchical structure, but "three paired relationships in which in each case one party is the *kephale* [head] of the other."[62] The main point becomes not a chain of command but divinely ordered differentiation. Giles concludes, "First Corinthians 11:3 is a difficult text to understand, but to interpret it to mean that the Father eternally has authority over the Son is unconvincing. Such an idea is nowhere else suggested by Paul."[63]

Letham agrees with Giles that this passage is so debated that it cannot be used to definitively sway the argument. He says,

> Giles is right to argue against undue reliance on 1 Corinthians 11:3 on the grounds that it is a difficult text to interpret. This should apply whatever the conclusions one reaches on its meaning. If a case has to be constructed, one way or the other, on this passage it is a weak case from the first.[64]

Yet Letham does not explicitly say the passage cannot be used in support of the totality of biblical witness, but only that it should not be used as though it were the *only* argument for the Son's eternal submission. Certainly, it may be used in cooperation with the broad witness of Scripture to support what is spelled out more clearly in the other texts reviewed in this chapter.

The main question I want to address in this section is whether this verse is looking solely to the relationship between God and

---

60. Giles, *Jesus and Father*, 111–12.
61. Giles, *Jesus and Father*, 112.
62. Giles, *Jesus and Father*, 112.
63. Giles, *Jesus and Father*, 112.
64. Letham, "Reply to Kevin Giles," 339.

Eternal Submission

the incarnate Christ. On the use of 1 Corinthians 11:3 in support of ESS, Fred Sanders has written, "1 [Corinthians] 11:3 is not a shortcut. It's a bona fide hard passage, but mostly it's about the incarnation."[65] Is this the case? An examination of 1 Corinthians 11:3 will show that we can neither definitively prove nor disprove Jesus' eternal submission from this passage alone.

In 1 Corinthians 11, Paul appears to be giving instruction for maintaining appropriate roles within the church at Corinth. Verses 2–16 talk about retaining gender distinctions during worship in the church through the use of the head covering.[66] Verse 3 is vital to the passage because it presents the theological grounds upon which Paul builds his case. The first question that must be addressed asks what is meant by the term "head" (κεφαλή)? According to Grudem and Ware, κεφαλή in this context refers to authority.[67] Giles, on the other hand, believes it cannot mean authority,[68] although he does not offer an alternative meaning. How are we to understand κεφαλή in this passage?

Ciampa and Rosner summarize three possibilities for the term's meaning here: "source," "authority," or "preeminence."[69] Their analysis of the options is important to our discussion:

> Even if by "head" Paul means "more prominent/preeminent partner" or (less likely) "one through whom the other exists," his language and the flow of the argument seem to reflect an assumed hierarchy through which glory and shame flow upward from those with lower status to those above them.[70]

The point made above is that in this passage, improper worship ultimately brings shame not only to oneself but to God.

---

65. Sanders, "18 Theses."
66. Following Ciampa and Rosner, *First Letter*, 503–4.
67. Ware, *Father, Son,* 72; Grudem, *Systematic Theology*, 459–60.
68. Giles, *Jesus and Father*, 112.
69. Ciampa and Rosner, *First Letter*, 508.
70. Ciampa and Rosner, *First Letter*, 509.

A Biblical Examination of Eternal Submission

By bringing up God's relationship to Christ as his head Paul completes the line so that his following discussion about shaming one's head will be understood to have implications for bringing shame or honor to God, who stands at the top of the series of heads and is to be glorified and honored in the Corinthians' worship, not dishonored by it.[71]

Rather than being three pairings as Giles contests, 1 Corinthians 11:3 shows a hierarchical structure where God stands above all.

But does this hierarchy relate to God's relationship over Christ in his humanity or does it speak of an eternal ordering? There are several points to consider here. First, Paul's use of the term "Christ" without the modifying "Jesus" should be considered as relevant to our discussion. Second, Paul's conception of Christ's glorified condition and status at God's right hand would have informed his writing and understanding of the relationship between God and Christ on the one hand and men and women on the other.

First, it is important to note that the term "Christ" (Χριστός) occurs in this context without the normal modifying name "Jesus" (Ἰησοῦς). In Paul's writings this term, which is the Greek translation of the Hebrew title "Messiah," or "anointed one," generally applies to the humanity of Christ, or his human office of anointed one.[72] However, there are instances where it might be contested that this title applies not only to the economy of salvation but on a larger scale. In particular, Ephesians 1:10 should be examined to this effect. In Ephesians 1:10, Christ is viewed as the agent who will accomplish God's will (v. 9) and bring all things to completion, both things in heaven and things on earth. The title here appears to have a more comprehensive emphasis than the temporal, incarnate ministry of the eternal Son. This emphasis is revisited in Ephesians 3:4, where Paul speaks of the mystery of Christ, and then defines that mystery as God's plan for a renewed humanity initiated through the building of Christ's church. This mystery was "hidden

---

71. Ciampa and Rosner, *First Letter*, 507.
72. For a few examples see Rom 5:6, 8; 6:4, 8–9; 1 Cor 5:7; 15:3.

Eternal Submission

for ages in God" (Eph 3:9). Paul's use of Christ here in Ephesians seems to expand from the incarnate man to the eternally chosen Messiah. These texts at least indicate that there is room for Paul's use of Χριστός to expand beyond the normal boundaries of the incarnate Messiah. His use of Χριστός without Ἰησοῦς, therefore, is not a definitive argument.

Second, Paul's conceptualization of Christ as risen and seated at the right hand of God the Father should inform our understanding of his thinking about their relationship. Christ had died, God had raised him from the dead, and now he was seated at the right hand of the Father in heaven (Eph 1:20–23). Christ had been raised to glorified, endless life. He would continue to enjoy this resurrected life into the everlasting future (Eph 1:21, 1 Cor 15:24–28). Thus, the risen and glorified Christ is who Paul has in mind in 1 Corinthians 11:3 as the one who is head of every man, but who also has God (the Father) as his head. If the risen, glorified Christ continues to have God the Father as his authority in regard to the economy of salvation, yet this is not ultimately reflective of their immanent relationship, there seems to be a dangerous disconnect between the economic Trinity and immanent Trinity.

To conclude this discussion, in examining 1 Corinthians 11:3 two extremes should be avoided. First, the passage is not simply a trump card to be thrown down without careful examination and exegesis. It is a difficult passage, as Sanders rightly highlights, and should be approached with caution.[73] On the other hand, we must not dismiss or ignore the passage simply because it is a difficult one. Most likely Paul is setting up his argument to show God at the top of the pyramid of authority and Christ, in regard to both his humanity and eternality, submitting to that authority in a way that is analogous to men and women in the church. This passage, then, should not be used as the *primary* evidence for the eternal submission of the Son, but as *supportive* evidence that complements well other passages which have been examined.

---

73. Sanders, "18 Theses."

A Biblical Examination of Eternal Submission

Summary of Biblical Defense

In this chapter we have looked at several biblical passages which provide support for the doctrine of the eternal submission of the Son to the Father. These passages have yielded corresponding evidence at three main levels: (1) the relationship between the Father and the preincarnate Son (John 6:38–39; Heb 5:5–6; Phil 2:6–7), (2) the relationship between Father and the incarnate Son as a consistent and accurate reflection of their eternal relationship (John 6:38–39, Phil 2:7–8, 1 Cor 11:3), and (3) the post-resurrection and exaltation relationship between Father and Son, both in the present era (Heb 5:5–6) and in the future (1 Cor 15:24–28, Rev 1:1–2). We have also touched on some of the theological reasons as to why we cannot make a sharp distinction between the life of the eternal Son in the immanent Trinity and his actions in the economic Trinity. Chapter 5 will more carefully examine these considerations in its offering of a theological defense for the eternal submission of the Son. First, we turn to an examination of the history of interpretation of 1 Corinthians 15 to demonstrate the inability of church history to speak definitively to the question of eternal submission.

Chapter 4

The Witness of the Church and Eternal Submission

First Corinthians 15:20–28 as a Test Case

One common argument against the eternal submission of the Son is that it is a modern invention created in the twentieth century by those who were looking for added theological support for discussions of gender and church roles. Recently, opponents of ESS have sought to show that in the history of Trinitarian development within the early church, the church fathers do not speak about the Son as subordinate or submissive to the Father eternally, but only in relation to redemptive history. They claim that using ESS as a way to support gender distinctions within the church and marital relationships is heretical because it goes against the orthodox teaching of the church.

This line of reasoning relates to a more recent development in evangelical hermeneutics: the theological interpretation of Scripture. Theological interpretation of Scripture (TIS) seeks to explore a philosophy of biblical interpretation challenging modernist presuppositions about the nature of history and interpretation. By reclaiming ancient exegetical methods and drawing from the best of contemporary practices, TIS looks for scriptural interpretations

The Witness of the Church and Eternal Submission

not devoid of but infused with the Holy Spirit. "It is about unlearning our mastery over the biblical text and releasing it to be an instrument used by God for our transformation on the path of Jesus Christ."[1]

One of the major tenants of TIS is that Scripture should be read and interpreted not merely individually, but in community both as it relates to space (across geographic boundaries) and time (across the eras of church history). Scripture must be interpreted by the community of faith in the church.[2] The church is not merely defined as a local entity, but believers in Christ crossing geographical, social, and ethnic borders, as well as temporal borders. We must read the Scriptures along with Spirit-filled believers from all throughout the history of the church, not simply in our modern era or from the Reformation onward.[3] If ESS is a modern resurgence of a doctrine rejected by the larger witness of Christendom from patristic times onward, that realization *should* impact the way we view the doctrine and our interpretation of passages of Scripture that could be used to support it.

This leads us to the question at hand: did the early church fathers accept or reject the idea of the eternal submission of the Son in regard to his relationship with the Father? How was this concept viewed in medieval interpretation? Were the Reformers outspoken against ESS? The aim of this chapter is to show, contrary to what many are saying in the evangelical community today, there was *no general consensus* on the topic of the eternal relational submission of the Son to the Father in the history of the church. While some voices seem to oppose ESS, others appear to embrace it.

To accomplish this purpose, I will present a brief history of the interpretation of 1 Corinthians 15:20–28, which was examined exegetically in chapter 3, and which has been used in the modern era as one of several proof texts for ESS.[4] I will examine interpre-

---

1. Billings, *Word of God*, 29.

2. Bartholomew and Thomas, *A Manifesto*, 1–3. See also Billings, *Word of God*, 149–51.

3. See Billings, *Word of God*, 149–94 for his excellent chapter on "The Value of Premodern Biblical Interpretation."

4. See Ware, *Father, Son*, 83–84; Grudem, "Biblical Evidence," 251–54.

tations of this text from the patristic, medieval, and Reformation periods before commenting on the broader implications of this study for the contemporary Trinitarian debate.

First Corinthians 15:20–28 in Patristic Interpretation

During the patristic period, questions surrounding the Trinity were the hot topic of discussion. The Arian controversy of the fourth century brought Christ's position in relation to God the Father to the forefront of all thinking Christian minds. Yet this debate primarily concerned the *ontological* subordination of Christ and not his submission in terms of the *relations* between Father and Son. Some voices even made explicit that while ontologically Christ was equal to the Father, relationally he was begotten, sent, and submissive to his Father from eternity. This can be seen by an examination of patristic commentary on 1 Corinthians 15:20–28.

On the one hand, there were church fathers who, in an attempt to combat Arianism, attempted to speak of this passage as relating solely to the humanity of Christ and not his deity. In other words, Christ in his humanity offers the kingdom back to the Father and so is subject to him in humanity only. Theodoret of Cyr says of 1 Corinthians 15:27, "The Arians and Eunomians love to play with this and the next verse claiming that it proves that Christ is not God. But here they are confusing two different things. The apostle is not speaking about Christ in his divinity but about his humanity, since the whole discussion is about the resurrection of the flesh."[5]

Augustine likewise dichotomizes the person of Christ as a way to help interpret this passage. "The rule of Catholic faith is this: when the Scriptures say of the Son that he is less than the Father, the Scriptures mean in respect to the assumption of humanity. But

---

5. Bray, *1–2 Corinthians*, 163.

The Witness of the Church and Eternal Submission

when the Scriptures point out that he is equal, they are understood in respect to his deity."[6]

Chrysostom summarizes well the interpretation of this passage which suggests it relates only to the humanity of Christ:

> The apostle speaks in one way when he is talking about the Godhead alone and in another way when he is speaking about the divine dispensation. For example, once he has established the context of our Lord's incarnation, Paul is not afraid to talk about his many humiliations, because these are not inappropriate to the incarnate Christ, even though they obviously cannot apply to God. In the present context, which of these two is he talking about? Given that he has just mentioned Christ's death and resurrection, neither of which can apply to God, it is clear that he is thinking of the divine dispensation of the incarnation, in which the Son has willingly subjected himself to the Father.[7]

With voices like Theodoret, Augustine, and Chrysostom, should we not conclude that this was the consensus of the early church? That would be too hasty of an assertion.

Interpretations of 1 Corinthians 15:20–28 supporting ESS can be found dating back to the fourth century AD. Ambrosiaster in his commentary on 1 Corinthians repeatedly points to the Son being subordinate to the Father in role or function. In commenting on verses 24–27 he says,

> No one should doubt, therefore, that the Son will reign with his Father forever. This is the standard teaching about the kingdom, that once all things have been subject to the Son and they have worshiped him as God, and

---

6. Bray, *1–2 Corinthians*, 164. Although Augustine's commentary here does not explicitly bring out any ordering of the Trinitarian persons, Keith E. Johnson has shown that there does exist in his theology an ordered relationship between Father and Son. Johnson criticizes both opponents and proponents of ESS in that opponents "ignore or subtly deny this reality," while proponents are wrong in assigning to Augustine's ordering the idea of submission when the eternal generation of the Son was what constituted this ordering in his mind. Johnson, "Trinitarian Agency," 7–25.

7. Bray, *1–2 Corinthians*, 163.

Eternal Submission

once death has been destroyed, then Christ will make it clear to them that he is not the ultimate source of all things, but that it is only through him that all things exist. To hand over the kingdom to God the Father will be to show that the Father is the one *from whom all fatherhood in heaven and on earth is named.*[8]

Ambrosiaster goes on to further clarify the relationship between Father and Son:

> The Father has subjected everything to the Son in order for the Son to be honored in a way similar to that in which the Father is honored. Therefore, when everything has confessed that Christ is God and been subjected beneath his feet, Christ the Lord will also be made subject to God the Father, so that God may be all in all. What Paul is saying is that when the pride of all rulers and powers and dominions has been put down that they have all worshiped Christ as God, then even Christ, because of the Father's unique authority, will show that although he is God, he is also from God, so that the sublime and ineffable authority of the single originating principle may be preserved.[9]

In these two sections of his commentary, Ambrosiaster views God the Father as the "single originating principle" and the one "from whom all fatherhood in heaven and on earth is named." The Father possesses a "unique authority" which the Son, "although he is God," does not possess. Ambrosiaster did not regard this passage as only speaking about the humanity of Christ, but of his deity as well, and does not divide the two as sharply as Augustine and Chrysostom.

Cyril of Jerusalem, a fourth century AD theologian, also gives strong support to ESS in 1 Corinthians 15:28 when he says:

> The LORD says this to the Lord, not to a servant, but to the Lord of all, and His own Son, to whom He put all things in subjection. "But when He saith that all things

---

8. Ambrosiaster, *Commentaries*, 195. Emphasis mine.
9. Ambrosiaster, *Commentaries*, 195.

are put under Him, it is manifest that He is excepted, which did put all things under Him," and what follows; "that God may be all in all." The Only-begotten Son is Lord of all, but the obedient Son of the Father, for He grasped not the Lordship, but received it by nature of the Father's own will.[10]

Furthermore, Cyril says:

> For He shall be subjected, not because He shall then begin to do the Father's will (for from eternity He "doeth" always "those things that please him" [John 8:29] but because, then as before, He obeys the Father, yielding, not a forced obedience, but a self-chosen accordance; for He is not a servant, that He should be subjected by force, but a Son, that He should comply of His free choice and natural love.[11]

This conveys both the idea of voluntary submission on the part of the Son out of his "free choice and natural love," and the idea that this submission to the Father's will occurs in eternity.

While some early church fathers interpreted 1 Corinthians 15:20–28 as referring only to the humanity of Christ, others interpreted these verses as referring to the order that exists within the Godhead eternally where the Father is in some way the source of the Son's power and authority.[12] Among church fathers of the patristic period there was no harmonious agreement either rejecting or accepting the eternal relational subordination of the Son from this passage.

10. Cyril of Jerusalem, *Catechetical Letters*, 2.7:59.

11. Cyril of Jerusalem, *Catechetical Letters*, 2.7:113.

12. In his response to Gilbert Bilezikian's article "Hermeneutical Bungee-Jumping," Letham writes, "Bilezikian does not appear to realize that an order (*taxis*) among the persons is part of trinitarian orthodoxy. He states that after the Arian controversy 'order or ranking' is excluded among the persons 'concerning their eternal state.' He conflates two different concepts, one heretical, the other orthodox. The idea of rank is certainly heresy, of that we both agree . . . Basil and Gregory of Nyssa at times implied that the three persons constitute a causal chain, with the Father being fully God, and the two others deriving their deity from him. However, the true order is not a rank, but an orderly disposition." Letham, *Holy Trinity*, 482–83.

Eternal Submission

First Corinthians 15:20–28 in Medieval Interpretation

During the medieval period (from about the fifth century AD up to the Reformation) there appears to be only limited advances of patristic thought in regard to the relationship of the Father and Son from 1 Corinthians 15:20–28. Trinitarian development in this era was sparse at best, and interpretations of 1 Corinthians are even more difficult to find. There are, however, several important points to discuss here.

First, a few broader comments should be made regarding ESS and Trinitarian thought during this time. Thomas Aquinas was the most prominent theologian of the thirteenth century. In many ways, his thought continued in the Augustinian tradition. Kevin Giles believes that Aquinas completely rejected subordination in any form. "With his stress on the divine unity of the Godhead, it is inconceivable for him that the Son and the Spirit might be subordinate in any way."[13] Yet even within Giles' discussion Aquinas is quoted as saying, "For among divine persons there is a kind of *natural order* but no *hierarchic order*."[14] This statement supports the idea of full equality for each person in the Trinity while at the same time a "natural" ordering with the Father primary.

On 1 Corinthians 15:28 specifically, Aquinas at first says, "These words are to be understood of Christ's human nature, wherein He is less than the Father, and subject to Him; but in His divine nature He is equal to the Father."[15] However, he goes on to cite Hilary of Poitier's *De Synodis*: "'The Son subjects Himself by His inborn piety'—that is, by His recognition of paternal authority; whereas 'creatures are subject by their created weakness.'"[16] The

---

13. Giles, *Jesus and Father*, 160.

14. Giles, *Jesus and Father*, 160. Emphasis mine. Giles references Aquinas, *Summa Theologica*, 1.108.1.

15. Aquinas, *Summa Theologica*, 1.42.4.

16. Aquinas, *Summa Theologica*, 1.42.4. Hilary elsewhere states, "God is One on account of the true character of His natural essence and because from the Unborn God the Father, who is the one God, the Only-begotten God the Son is born, and draws His divine Being only from God; and since the essence

The Witness of the Church and Eternal Submission

phrase "paternal authority" is contrasted with the phrase "creatures are subject by their created weakness." In other words, the Son subjects himself because of his relationship to the Father and a pious recognition of the Father's "paternal authority."

Is he speaking of this authority in terms of the human Christ in relation to his Father, or the eternal Son? It is likely he is referring to their eternal relations because, in the next section, Aquinas argues that the Father and Son have the same essence and dignity. This is shown in different ways between Father and Son.

> Therefore, paternity is the Father's dignity, as also the Father's essence: since dignity is something absolute, and pertains to the essence. As, therefore, the same essence, which in the Father is paternity, in the Son is filiation, so the same dignity which, in the Father is paternity, in the Son is filiation. It is thus true to say that the Son possesses whatever dignity the Father has . . . For the Father and the Son have the same essence and dignity, which exist in the Father by the relation of giver, and in the Son by the relation of receiver.[17]

Aquinas shows the unity of Father and Son in possession of the same essence and dignity, but the distinction of persons in that these exist in the Father "by the relation of giver," and in the Son "by the relation of receiver." Eternal generation is in view here, but

---

of Him who is begotten is exactly similar to the essence of Him who begat Him, there must be one name for the exactly similar nature. That the Son is not on a level with the Father and is not equal to Him is chiefly shewn in the fact that He was subjected to Him to render obedience, in that the Lord rained from the Lord and that the Father did not, as Photinus and Sabellius say, rain from Himself, as the Lord from the Lord; in that He then sat down at the right hand of God when it was told Him to seat Himself; in that He is sent, in that He receives, in that He submits in all things to the will of Him who sent Him. But the subordination of filial love is not a diminution of essence, nor does pious duty cause a degeneration of nature, since in spite of the fact that both the Unborn Father is God and the Only-begotten Son of God is God, God is nevertheless One, and the subjection and dignity of the Son are both taught in that by being called Son He is made subject to that name which because it implies that God is His Father is yet a name which denotes His nature." Hilary of Poitiers, *De Synodis*, 2.9a:18.

17. Aquinas, *Summa Theologica*, 1.42.4.

Eternal Submission

along with it, elements of paternal authority, the Father as giver, and the Son as receiver. While Aquinas does not explicitly endorse an eternal submission of the Son in 1 Corinthians 15, neither does he entirely close the door on the idea.[18]

Richard of Saint Victor likewise affirms that there is no distinction between the persons in terms of their possession of deity, but there is a distinction in persons in terms of their *origin*. "The Son, whom [the Father] had from eternity, has been eternally begotten, and with reason we must say that he has eternally received being. Therefore, he is called 'begotten'; and not even just begotten, but also 'only-begotten,' since in the Trinity there is only one Son."[19] Both Aquinas and Richard of Saint Victor are very systematic and rational in their approach rather than being concerned primarily to comment on the biblical text itself. Yet they both hold to the ontological equality of Father and Son eternally, and at the same time maintain a distinction between persons in their relations based on origin (only the Son is eternally begotten).

We are not, however, limited to making broad Trinitarian claims during this period without ability to speak to our passage. Oecumenius wrote a commentary on Paul's epistles somewhere between the sixth and ninth centuries AD.[20] Commenting on 1 Corinthians 15:27, he says, "The things of the Son belong to God as Father, and everything which the Son can do is attributed to the

---

18. Aquinas later says, "As the same essence is paternity in the Father, and filiation in the Son: so by the same power the Father begets, and the Son is begotten. Hence it is clear that the Son can do whatever the Father can do; yet it does not follow that the Son can beget; for to argue thus would imply transition from substance to relation, for generation signifies a divine relation. So the Son has the same omnipotence as the Father, but with another relation; the Father possessing power as *giving* signified when we say that He is able to beget; while the Son possesses the power of *receiving*, signified by saying that He can be begotten." Aquinas, *Summa Theologica*, 1.42.6. This statement reveals that Aquinas allowed for one divine power "possessed" in different ways by the Father and Son.

19. Angelici, *Richard of Saint Victor*, 222.

20. Traditionally thought to have written several commentaries in the ninth century, recent scholarship has redated Oecumenius' *Commentary on the Apocalypse* to the late sixth or early seventh centuries.

The Witness of the Church and Eternal Submission

Father, for *he who begot him outside time is the source of the Son's power.*"[21] Here, Oecumenius claims that God the Father eternally begot the Son outside of time (in the immanent Trinity), and is the source of the Son's power not only in the incarnation, but eternally. This points toward the idea of there being an order (*taxis*) among the members of the Trinity, not in terms of rank, but in terms of relation.[22] The Father is the authoritarian as the source of the Son's power. The Son is relationally submissive in that he receives power from his Father.[23] For Oecumenius, the eternal generation of the Son implies in some sense a submissive role in relation to his Father, for the Father is the *source* or giver of the Son's power, and the Son is the recipient of that power.[24]

While Trinitarian thought during the medieval period was not largely advanced, we can see from Thomas Aquinas, Richard of St. Victor, and Oecumenius that there was no received rule of faith that demanded either the acceptance or denial of ESS. There was room in this era for discussions of the distinctions of the Trinitarian persons in terms of their origin. While these discussions did not explicitly affirm the Son's eternal submission to the Father in role or relation, neither did they rule it out as heretical, as some would propagate.[25]

---

21. Bray, *1–2 Corinthians*, 163. Emphasis mine.

22. Letham says this idea of an order in the Trinity in terms of personal relations exists within Augustine's writings as well. Letham, *Holy Trinity*, 193.

23. Interestingly, Oecumenius also contrasts 1 Corinthians 15:27–28 with Greek mythology: "Paul is writing to converted Greeks, because the Greeks worshiped Zeus, who revolted against his own father in order to seize his kingdom. He was concerned lest they should imagine something similar in the case of Christ and his Father." Bray, *1–2 Corinthians*, 163.

24. Contra Giles, who argues that eternal generation does not imply eternal relational subordination, and the two must be kept separate. Giles, *Eternal Generation*, 231–33.

25. Giles, *Jesus and Father*, 160.

Eternal Submission

The Reformers and 1 Corinthians 15:20–28

Moving on to the Reformation period and beyond, the same trend of no clear-cut consensus regarding the Son's subjection to the Father is evident. John Calvin, in looking at 1 Corinthians 15:20–28, says:

> But Christ will then hand back the Kingdom which He has received, so that we may cleave completely to God. This does not mean that He will abdicate from the Kingdom in this way, but will transfer it in some way or other (*quodammodo*) from His humanity to His glorious divinity, because then there will open up for us a way of approach, from which we are now kept back by our weakness. In this way, therefore, Christ will be subjected to the Father, because, when the veil has been removed, we will see God plainly, reigning in His majesty, and the humanity of Christ will no longer be in between us to hold us back from a nearer vision of God.[26]

In assessing Calvin's take, Letham writes, "His comments on [1 Corinthians 15:27–28] have a definitely Nestorian ring to them."[27] He continues:

> At the conclusion of his mediatorial kingdom, Calvin says, Christ will hand the kingdom back to God. He will not abdicate his kingship in any way, "but will transfer it in some way or other from his humanity to his glorious divinity." This seems to imply a division in the person of Christ. Indeed, he goes on to say that we will then see God plainly in his majesty, "and the humanity of Christ will no longer be in between us to hold us back from a nearer vision of God." This astonishing statement appears to conflict with Calvin's otherwise strong, and definitely orthodox, focus on the Incarnation. It is as if in attempting to guard against any diminution of Christ's full deity, he has momentarily lost his grasp of the union of the two natures of the incarnate Christ.[28]

---

26. Calvin, *First Epistle*, 327.
27. Letham, *Holy Trinity*, 255.
28. Letham, *Holy Trinity*, 255–256. Indeed, Calvin's take on this verse is in

The Witness of the Church and Eternal Submission

Calvin's comments show that in his thinking there is a continuity between the mediatorial kingdom of Christ and his eternal rule, yet the emphasis in eternity is on Christ's deity.

There is a problem here of making too sharp of a distinction between Christ's humanity and his deity. Letham charges Calvin as being close to Nestorianism and makes a point which should be considered not only in regard to Calvin, but also to interpreters of this passage throughout the church's history. Does our understanding of the incarnation of Christ really allow us to view some passages as only being in reference to his humanity or his deity, as per Augustine? Or does the hypostatic union force us to see Christ's actions in his humanity as inseparable from and consistent with his divine eternal disposition? Apparently, Calvin struggled to understand the answer to these questions in his interpretation of this passage.

Luther's commentary on 1 Corinthians is instructive here as well. In commenting on 1 Corinthians 15:27–28, he speaks of Christ handing over his kingdom and subjecting himself to the Father eternally:

> This is what St. Paul calls delivering the Kingdom to the Father, that is, presenting us and His whole Christendom openly to the Father into *eternal clarity and glory*, that He Himself may reign without cloak or cover. But Christ will nevertheless retain His rule and majesty; for *He is the same God and Lord*, eternal and omnipotent with the Father... Everything must be subject to Him, "excepting Him who put all things under Him," until the Last Day. Then He will abolish all of this and subject Himself with His entire kingdom to the Father...[29]

Thus, Luther envisioned a future when the temporal kingdom of Christ would be given over to the Father "into eternal clarity and

---

many ways akin to Marcellus of Ancyra, who "solved the difficulties presented to [the Son's] generation by Prov 8:22 and 1 Cor 15:28 by applying the first to the incarnate Word and the second by his peculiar doctrine of the reabsorption after the rendering up of the kingdom of the *Logos* into God and the disappearance of the Son (i.e. of the human nature of the *Logos* when incarnate)." Hanson, *Search for Christian Doctrine*, 843.

29. Luther, "Commentary," 141. Emphasis mine.

glory," a reference to unending rule in eternity future. The subjection of Christ then continues for all eternity, since he would "subject Himself with His entire kingdom to the Father." It appears Luther was very comfortable assigning to the Son an eternal submission to the Father in role, while at the same time affirming their ontological unity.

Finally, in the post-Reformation, early American era Jonathan Edwards' notes on 1 Corinthians 15:28 tease at the idea of eternal submission. He begins by noting of Christ, "He is to be respected as God himself is, as supreme, and absolute, and sovereign Ruler."[30] For Edwards, clearly Christ is fully God. He concludes, however, by saying, "But with respect to government, God will be respected as Supreme Orderer, and Christ[31] with his church united to him and dependent on him, shall together be received of the benefit of his government."[32] Edwards regarded God the Father as "Supreme Orderer," and Christ in some way *depends* on him, being the receiver of benefits from the Father's government. This demonstrates an order of authority and submission in the Godhead.

In the Reformation period and following, some of the strongest theological voices supported the idea that Christ was fully God ontologically, but submissive to the Father in terms of their relationship. In their writings, Luther and Edwards give support to the eternal relational submission of the Son to the Father. This conclusion was arrived at in part by their interpretation of 1 Corinthians 15:20–28.

Implications for the Modern Trinitarian Debate

Both advocates and opponents of eternal relational submission point to church history as a means of supporting their arguments.

30. Edwards, *Notes on Scripture*, 95.

31. There is a note in the text that Edwards scratched out which originally said, "as subordinate unto him together" at this point. Edwards, *Notes on Scripture*, 96.

32. Edwards, *Notes on Scripture*, 96.

The Witness of the Church and Eternal Submission

Speaking against ESS, Kevin Giles boldly asserts, "The great theologians of the past, the creeds, and the Reformation confessions gave no support to the idea that the Son of God is eternally subordinate to the Father; indeed they passionately opposed this teaching."[33] We have seen that statements like these are inaccurate and misleading. Throughout the history of the church, from patristic times through the Reformation and beyond, there have been interpreters of 1 Corinthians 15:20–28 who have affirmed the ontological equality of the Father and Son while simultaneously maintaining a relational ordering where the Father has primacy and the Son submits. We cannot conclude that the uniform witness of orthodox Christianity, or even the teaching of "the best of theologians across the centuries,"[34] has been to reject the relational submission of the Son to the Father in eternity.

On the other hand, the evidence does not weigh so heavily in support of ESS that we could conclude "the eternal subordination of the Son is an orthodox doctrine believed from the history of the early church to the present day."[35] For example, H. Wayne House concludes his article on ESS in patristic thought with the following:

> Apart from a few early exceptions in the second century as the nature of the Trinity was being developed, the witness of the early church on the issue of role subordination is not fragmented or ambiguous. Rather, there is a centuries-long chorus in both east and west that the Son and Father are of the same essence. At the same time, however, the orthodox fathers believed that this did not prevent divine persons from being distinguished as to the relationship of God the Father, the unbegotten from all eternity and that of the eternally begotten Son, God of very God. The evidence is convincing that the early church never had any difficulty with knowing the difference between a heretical subordination of the Son to the Father in which they shared unequally the same divine

---

33. Giles, *Jesus and Father*, 170–71.
34. Giles, *Jesus and Father*, 129.
35. Kovach and Schemm, "Defense of Doctrine," 464.

Eternal Submission

> nature from the view that the Son is subordinate, of second order, in eternity with the Father as to their personal association based on the innate properties of Father and Son.[36]

This statement, while perhaps true of *some* church fathers, cannot be applied categorically across the board, because while many affirm the distinction of the Father and Son in terms of eternal generation, not all make explicit the connection between eternal generation and authority/submission. In 1 Corinthians 15:20–28 particularly, not all interpreters are convinced that Paul's words about Christ's subjection to the Father have eternal connotations. Rather, it seems at times for the church fathers quite the opposite is true.

It is best to take something of a mediating position in regards to 1 Corinthians 15:20–28 specifically, and by way of implication in regards to the question of ESS in church history as a whole. In this passage, our brief study of the history of interpretation shows some believed Christ's subjection to God the Father referred to Christ's humanity only, while others acknowledged some kind of eternal application. There was *no clear consensus* among the community of faith. What has been shown to be true of 1 Corinthians 15:20–28 specifically is also true of the entire issue more broadly. There was no agreed-upon dogma concerning the eternal relational submission of Jesus the Son to his Father, whether in support of or in opposition to the doctrine. It is quite probable that this issue was not fully formed in their minds the way it is in our modern Trinitarian debate.

Michael J. Ovey warns against dangers of misusing church history in the debate over eternal subordination. He says,

> The superordination of the Father was not the immediate issue. Care should be taken over imposing anachronistic questions onto the fourth-century debate, especially when presuppositions about the legitimacy or otherwise

---

36. House, "Eternal Relational Subordination," 178–79.

of power and authority can be so very different in our own era.[37]

At the end of his article assessing Augustine's writings in relation to ESS, Keith E. Johnson makes an excellent point about the engagement of modern Trinitarian scholars with the church fathers for the present debate:

> "Are you for us or for our adversaries?" asked Joshua when he encountered an imposing stranger bearing a sword outside the city of Jericho. "Neither," said the stranger, "I am the commander of the Lord's army." Perhaps we can learn a lesson from Joshua's encounter. In our quest to answer a speculative theological question, we can become so preoccupied with the question of whose side Augustine is on that we no longer let one of the church's leading theologians speak on his own terms . . . As we seek to understand scriptural teaching about the Trinity, the church fathers represent an invaluable resource. However, if we engage the fathers simply to determine whose "side" they are on—like pawns in a chess match—not only will we misinterpret them, but we may also fail to hear the ways in which they rightly challenge and correct our thinking about the Trinity.[38]

In sum, 1 Corinthians 15:20–28 shows a lack of uniformity in interpretation throughout the history of the church in speaking to the eternal subordination of the Son in role, and this is reflective of the relationship between ESS and the church fathers more broadly. Far from being the nail in the coffin of ESS, as some would convey, the evidence of church history shows in this passage a variety of interpretations and no general agreement one way or the other. This does not mean that voices from the community of faith throughout the ages should not be appealed to in the ESS debate. Rather, theologians on both sides of the debate should realize wide-ranging claims of universal ecclesio-historical support

---

37. Ovey, "True Sonship," 130.
38. Johnson, "Trinitarian Agency," 25.

for their position do not align with the evidence and are ultimately unhelpful.

Theological interpretation of Scripture, in presenting the necessity of reading Scripture along with Spirit-filled Christians in ages past, offers an important exegetical tool that should be taken up and mastered by students of God's word today. Kevin Giles says the same when he writes, "The best guide to a right interpretation of the Scriptures in relation to any historically developed doctrine is the theological tradition, especially given in creeds and confessions."[39] I fully agree. However, in the case of ESS, I have argued there is no uniform theological tradition. TIS is not, however, limited to hearing only the voices of church fathers, but also encompasses both careful exegetical examinations of individual texts, and theological examinations of those texts in light of the broader canon of Scripture. If church history cannot decisively affirm or deny ESS, we must look to biblical and theological studies for more definitive answers. Scholars on both sides, then, must stop citing the church fathers as their death blow to the other side. The battle over eternal submission will not be won on the field of church history, but rather in the trenches of biblical and theological studies.

---

39. Giles, *Eternal Generation*, 57.

Chapter 5

A Theological Examination of Eternal Submission

IN CHAPTER THREE WE looked at several biblical passages which, I have argued, show the eternal submission of the Son to the Father. In this chapter we turn to theological arguments which have been raised against ESS by contemporary theologians. For each argument below I will present the questions raised against ESS and then offer a theological response to the question or problem. While not every theological issue pertaining to eternal submission can be addressed by this limited study, I have attempted to select and examine theological issues that both occur frequently in recent Trinity debates and are, in my estimation, most significant.[1]

Eternal Submission, Divine Unity, and Divine Authority

The question is raised by a number of individuals who oppose the eternal submission of the Son: if Jesus is fully God, and one with

---

1. These six issues were chosen from my reading and review of both printed and online material related to ESS. Variations of these arguments occur often throughout the blog posts in particular. For an extensive listing of blogs from the 2016 Trinitarian debate, see Jeffery, "2016 Trinity Debate."

Eternal Submission

God the Father in authority and power, how can God submit to God? The danger here, it is argued, is that if the Son is eternally submissive to the Father, the logical conclusion is that he is a lesser god than the Father. Kevin Giles warns of this problem when he writes:

> I argue that to teach that the Son must always obey the Father, that he is eternally subordinated in authority to the Father, also implies his ontological subordination. If the Son must always obey the Father, he is not the Father's equal in power. What makes God God is his omnipotence—his absolute power. If Jesus is not omnipotent in exactly the same way as the Father because he is eternally set under the Father's authority, then he is not fully God.[2]

Said another way, eternal submission does too much to threaten the divine unity of the Trinity through making an unbiblical distinction between the persons.

Millard Erickson, an evangelical egalitarian, takes a similar view when he writes:

> One way of characterizing these two different views is to say that on the gradational view [his term for ESS], the Son is necessarily subordinate to the Father. He could not be otherwise. Under any and all circumstances (or as it is sometimes put in philosophical discussions, "in all possible worlds"), the Father has authority over the Son and the Son is subordinate to the Father.[3]

Thus, we see these two theologians arguing that any sort of relational subordination from the Son to the Father destroys divine unity and in effect transforms the Trinitarian persons into distinct "gods." The Son is not as much God as God the Father because he has no choice but to submit and obey in their intra-Trinitarian relationship.

---

2. Giles, *Jesus and Father*, 59.
3. Erickson, *Who's Tampering?*, 171.

A Theological Examination of Eternal Submission

Egalitarian opponents to eternal submission are not the only ones raising this important issue. Liam Goligher put the matter similarly when he wrote:

> It comes down to this; if they [advocates of ESS] are right we have been worshipping an idol since the beginning of the church; and if they are wrong they are constructing a new deity—a deity in whom there are degrees of power, differences of will, and diversity of thought. Because, mark this, to have an eternally subordinate Son intrinsic to the Godhead creates the potential of three minds, wills and powers.[4]

Goligher continues, "And John is wrong when He says that 'the Word is God,' for, by definition, if He is a servant bound to obey, then He must not have as much Godness as God the Father has in . . . Himself."[5] His point is that Jesus as the eternal Son cannot be both eternally submissive and at the same time *fully* God. He must in some way be an inferior deity.

Does relational submission[6] effectively subordinate the Son ontologically? Is the Father more God, the Son a little less God, and the Spirit lesser still? Goligher contests that this is the case, and in response offers his view of how the Trinity should be seen:

> In the repose of their eternal life, the divine persons shared one mind, one will, one power, because there is but one God (and not three) with one divine nature (Phil. 2, Col. 1, Heb. 1), one divine splendor, and one divine being. The relations are signaled by the names ascribed to them: The Father begetting the Son (Psalm 2, John 1), the Son being the begotten, and the Spirit proceeding as the mutual love of the Father and the Son. These eternal relations, absolutely considered, pertain to being: the Son and Spirit share the very nature of God as God—they are essentially identical (though relatively

---

4. Goligher, "Is it Okay?"
5. Goligher, "Is it Okay?"
6. I am using the term "relational submission" here as a synonym for eternal submission. The Son is submissive to the Father eternally as it relates to their personal relationship, not ontologically as it relates to the divine nature.

Eternal Submission

distinct). Within this eternal life, there was distinction without primacy and order of being without priority of life or authority.[7]

In response, I contend that Jesus is eternally submissive to his Father in their intra-Trinitarian relationship, and at the same time possesses full deity. There are several reasons that lead to this conclusion.

First, eternal submission is proper to the *personhood* of the Son, not the divine *essence*. Relational submission does not necessitate ontological submission. When talking about the Trinity, theologians distinguish between divine identity (the oneness of God, his unity) and divine diversity (the threeness of God, personal distinctions).[8] Both are vital to who God is, and the two aspects of triune life are not contradictory. Scott Swain calls these two aspects of divine life "common and personal properties." He says,

> The twofold description of the [Trinitarian] persons exhibited in Matthew 11:25–27, and also in many other biblical texts, constitutes the fundamental biblical basis for the doctrine of the Trinity. The Bible identifies the persons with characteristics each person holds in common with the other persons ("common properties"), and with characteristics each person holds in distinction from the other persons ("personal properties").[9]

The two aspects of divine life are related to one another but are not ultimately equal to one another. If they were equal to one another, we would have one God assuming different forms without real and true distinctions between those forms, resulting in the heresy of Sabellianism or modalism. It is, therefore, legitimate to speak of aspects of the Trinity that relate to divine unity, and other aspects that relate to divine diversity.

---

7. Goligher, "Is it Okay?"

8. For a few examples see Berkhof, *Systematic Theology*, 89; Grudem, *Systematic Theology*, 231–41; Letham, *Holy Trinity*, 17–88.

9. Swain, "Mystery of Trinity," 216.

A Theological Examination of Eternal Submission

A case in point is the issue of eternal generation, which will be more fully examined below.[10] At this juncture, it will be sufficient to show that the Son's eternal generation from the Father reveals a relational distinction between the two persons that allow us to talk about them distinctly. The Father is not eternally generated, nor does the Son eternally generate another person. The distinction of eternal generation reveals that we are able to talk about relational distinctions and still maintain divine unity. Just because the Father eternally generates the Son does not necessitate that the Son is a lesser being. We are talking about two different aspects of God's divine life. To use an analogy, we could view God's essence and relations as two rails which make up a railroad track. They run parallel and complementary to one another, and ultimately work together in unity, yet are unwaveringly distinct—so are the divine essence and the divine relations.

Second, eternal submission does not necessitate a hierarchy within the Godhead, where the Father is ultimately greater than the Son. Many opponents of ESS have strongly asserted if any distinction is made in authority between Father and Son, then the theologian in question has moved away from Nicene Trinitarianism and orthodoxy.[11] Yet theologians who advocate that ESS demands a hierarchy of authority confuse the divine essence with the divine relations.

To talk about authority as it relates to God presents two possibilities. One could speak either of authority in relation to the divine essence/unity of the persons, or it could be authority in terms of the distinctions between the persons. The two are not synonymous; the first relates properly to the oneness of God, while the second relates to his threeness. There is one shared divine authority of God, and this authority is displayed from the one God *externally* toward all other things/persons in the economy of salvation. It is an external authority, then, in that it is the authority

---

10. For a good overview and explanation of eternal generation, see Sanders, *Deep Things*, 96–98.

11. Goligher, "Is it Okay?"; Goligher, "Reinventing God." Trueman, "Fahrenheit 381." See especially: Giles, *Jesus and Father*, 172–204.

of God viewed by those outside of God. There is also an *internal* range of authority within and among the persons of the Godhead as evidenced in Scripture.[12] In the way that they relate to one another, the Father possesses absolute authority and the Son submits to that authority. Externally, however, both Trinitarian persons share supreme authority.

This interplay between external divine authority and internal divine authority can be demonstrated biblically in several passages. In Philippians 2:9–11, Jesus is highly exalted and given the name above every name, so that all human beings throughout creation will bow before him in a future day. This again shows the external authority of the Son as fully God in himself, and so possessing all the power and authority of the triune God. Yet at the same time there is an eternal, intra-Trinitarian element of authority alluded to here. It is God (the Father) who exalts the Son and bestows on him the name above every name in verse 9. This reveals elements of the internal authority structure between Father and Son, with Father possessing ultimate authority and Son submissive to that authority for at least two reasons. First, the economic Trinitarian relationship between Father and Son is an accurate and consistent reflection of their immanent relationship.[13] If the Father possesses authority to give to the Son in the economy, it must have a consistent eternal corollary.

Second, what takes place in the economy in the Father exalting the Son at the resurrection and giving him the name above every name in creation has an enduring, everlasting aspect.[14] One day in the future, every knee will bow and every tongue will confess Jesus Christ is Lord, and from that point on, that state of exaltation will continue. So, into the eternal future Jesus Christ still possesses

---

12. See chapter 3 above for biblical support.

13. As per Rahner's Rule: see the next section below for an expanded explanation of immanent and economic consistency.

14. Melick, Jr., *Philippians, Colossians*, 108–9. Melick, Jr. says, "This is an eschatological picture. The hymn brings the future into view by describing the culmination of history, when all persons will acknowledge Jesus' lordship." Melick, Jr., *Philippians, Colossians*, 108–9.

A Theological Examination of Eternal Submission

a name and an authority that is *given* to him by his Father.[15] In other words, the authority structure demonstrated in the economy continues into the eternal, unending future.

Matthew 28:18 also demonstrates these dual aspects of divine authority: "And Jesus came up and spoke to them, saying, 'All authority has been given to Me in heaven and on earth.'" In his final post-resurrection appearance to the disciples in Matthew, Jesus appears and reveals to his disciples that he possesses all authority in heaven and on earth. This is the divine Trinitarian authority of God in his essence, absolute and total, in respect to what is external to him. At the same time, Jesus speaks of this authority as something that was given (ἐδόθη) to him in the past. He has taken possession of this divine authority, which was given to him by the Father.[16] This would relate to their intra-Trinitarian authority structure, where the Father possesses all authority and the Son submits to the Father. Yet in reference to the created universe, Jesus can say that he possesses all authority; there is no authority that does not belong to him. Matthew 28 shows both an internal authority structure between Jesus and the Father, and yet also one absolute divine authority which both Father and Son possess mutually.

Finally, in Ephesians 1:20, Paul speaks of the Father as the one who "raised Christ from the dead and seated him at his right hand in the heavenly realms." This is the highest place or position in the universe, at the right hand of God the Father. So Christ, in his relation to all created things, occupies the highest position. And yet within the heavenly throne room where the Trinitarian persons forever dwell, the apostle presents us with the image of

---

15. Melick, Jr. points out these elements of *external* and *internal* authority when he says, "Christ acted selflessly to accomplish the will of God. He even died to provide salvation as a part of the divine plan [internal authority]. God chose to honor him, determining that Christ would be the focus of the Godhead in its interactions with creation [external authority]. Because of Jesus' actions, the way to honor God is to honor Christ [external authority]. Even so, the glory Christ receives is a glory given to the Father [internal authority]. Again, a shared servanthood works to the mutual benefit of all involved." Melick, Jr., *Philippians, Colossians*, 108–9.

16. The Father's role as the giver of this authority is implicit here, and perhaps also in v. 19 with the ordering of the persons: Father, Son, and Holy Spirit.

God the Father enthroned and Jesus the Son sitting at his right hand.[17] This imagery presents us with a view of Jesus that is closely identified with God the Father (demonstrating divine unity), but at the same time distinct from him, as the Father is the one who raises Jesus from the dead and seats him at his right hand (showing their personal distinction). That Jesus is seated at the right hand of the Father in heaven is a recurring theme in the NT.[18]

Jesus as the eternal Son can be submissive to the Father in their intra-Trinitarian relations and at the same time maintain full deity. This is because we can talk about the distinctions between the persons in a way that is separate from the unity of the divine essence, as demonstrated by use of the term "eternal generation." The eternal Son can at the same time both possess all the authority of the Godhead in relation to the created world (external authority) and also yield to the authority of his Father within their intra-Trinitarian relationship (internal authority). Jesus can eternally submit to the Father relationally and simultaneously be fully God.

Eternal Submission and the Immanent-Economic Consistency of the Son

Another recurring criticism of ESS is that it confuses the immanent Trinity (God in himself apart from creation) and the economic Trinity (God as he works within creation). Goligher has put it bluntly:

---

17. Even if Paul's language here is analogous, the referent still demonstrates a divine and absolute authority that Christ possesses in respect to the created order (external authority), while showing levels of authority in the heavenly throne room where the Father's power and authority are primary and the Son's are in some way secondary (internal authority).

18. Eph 1:11 should be read in conjunction with John 17:5, where Jesus says, "Now, Father, glorify Me together with Yourself, with the glory which I had with You before the world was." Jesus' resurrection glory and seating at the right hand of the Father describes in some way a restoration of the glory which Jesus formerly possessed before his incarnation. Thus, his position in heaven at the Father's right hand is not solely an incarnate or post-incarnate position, but reflects in some way his eternal position.

A Theological Examination of Eternal Submission

> They [advocates of ESS] are building their case by reinventing the doctrine of God, and are doing so without telling the Christian public what they are up to. What we have is in fact a departure from biblical Christianity as expressed in our creeds and confessions. Out of that redefinition of God their teaching is being used to promote a new way of looking at human relationships which is more like Islam than Christianity; more concerned with control and governance than with understanding the nuances of the relationship of the Son with His Father in eternity on the one hand and how that differs from the roles they adopt in the economy of redemption on the other. They make this move by failing to distinguish between God as He is in Himself (ontology) and God as He is in Christ in outworking of the plan of redemption (economy).[19]

He explicitly states, "They collapse the intra-Trinitarian life of God into the roles adopted by the persons to accomplish our redemption."[20] For Goligher, the incarnate life of God the Son is not to be equated with his eternal life. "The incarnate Christ sets an example of godly living as God in human flesh; He does not give us an example of the eternal life of God."[21]

To respond to this strong criticism we need to examine several points. First, how do we define the terms "immanent" and "economic" Trinity? The works of Fred Sanders will contribute significantly toward this discussion. Second, what is the relationship between the immanent and economic Trinity? Karl Rahner's influence in this area will be an important point of discussion. Third, based on the first two points, can we legitimately separate the relationship of the Father and Son in the economy from their eternal relationship? The revelation of God in Christ and the danger of Nestorianism will weigh in here. All these points will work toward showing that Christ as the eternal Son acts only in such a way in the incarnation that is consistent with his eternal character and

---

19. Goligher, "Is it Okay?"
20. Goligher, "Is it Okay?"
21. Goligher, "Is it Okay?"

Eternal Submission

personhood. Thus, if the Son submits to the Father in the incarnation, he is acting in a way that is consistent and not contentious with or contradictory to his eternal disposition.

First, how should we define the "immanent Trinity" and the "economic Trinity?" Trinitarian scholar Fred Sanders says,

> The path we have traced from the salvation-historical missions to the relations of origin and back arcs across the vast distinction between God's actions in the world and God's eternal being. It could be described as connecting the Trinity we experience in salvation history (the sending Father, the incarnate Son Jesus Christ, and the Holy Spirit of Pentecost) with the Trinity of God's own eternal being (the Father who has not yet sent and will only do so by grace, the Son who has not yet become incarnate and will only do so by condescension, and the Holy Spirit who is not yet poured out and will only be so on the basis of the finished work of Christ). We could describe the entire project in other words as negotiating the relationship between the economic Trinity and the immanent Trinity. This is the conventional terminology of modern trinitarianism, widely used and thoroughly discussed.[22]

To unpack this paragraph, the economic Trinity is the one "we experience in salvation history," and the immanent Trinity is "God's own eternal being." It could be said that the difference between the two, from a human perspective, is that we only experience the economic Trinity because of our place in the created world and salvation history. Another way to state this, in terms similar to our above discussion, is that the immanent Trinity is the *internal* life of God as he is in himself, while the economic Trinity is the *external* life and actions of God displayed in the created world.

The next area that must be explored is the relationship between the immanent and the economic Trinity. Here again, the work of Fred Sanders is invaluable to this discussion. In the chapter "God Who Sends God" in *The Triune God*, Sanders gives a brief history of the terms from their first use under Johann August

---

22. Sanders, *Triune God*, 144.

A Theological Examination of Eternal Submission

Urlsperger, through their more widespread acknowledgement via Karl Rahner, down to their usage by modern Trinitarian theologians.[23] He contends Rahner's Rule, that the economic Trinity is the immanent Trinity and vice versa,[24] "has become the symbolic figurehead for modern use of the terms *economic Trinity* and *immanent Trinity*."[25] Sanders also presents some of the problems with the use of these terms:

> What is peculiar about its construction is that it verbally doubles the Trinity. While nobody thinks there are two actual trinities involved in reality, the reduplicative phrasing puts two trinities into any sentence framed by economic and immanent.[26]

What is the correlation between God's life in himself and God's life in relation to humanity? It is generally agreed today that the economic Trinity cannot simply be equated with the immanent Trinity.[27] Sanders argues that the economic Trinity is "the image of the immanent Trinity."[28] Giles devotes much attention to the modern discussion over this issue.[29] He summarizes the conclusion of many evangelicals when he writes, "There is correspondence but not identity [between the economic and immanent Trinity]. The triune God is not other than he reveals himself, but historical revelation never captures fully the divine reality."[30] Giles then concludes from this that "it is necessary and imperative that we do

---

23. Sanders, *Triune God*, 144–53.

24. Rahner, *Trinity*, 22. Rahner also said, "We are sure that the following statement is true: that no adequate distinction can be made between the doctrine of the Trinity and the doctrine of the economy of salvation." Rahner, *Trinity*, 22.

25. Sanders, *Triune God*, 148.

26. Sanders, *Triune God*, 145.

27. See Giles, *Jesus and Father*, 250–53; Sanders, *Triune God*, 144–53 for brief assessments of Rahner's rule.

28. Sanders, *Image of Immanent*.

29. Giles, *Jesus and Father*, 242–74.

30. Giles, *Jesus and Father*, 265.

Eternal Submission

not read back the Son's subordination in the economy of salvation into the eternal or immanent Trinity."[31]

I fully agree that there is "correspondence but not identity" between the economic and immanent aspects of the Trinity.[32] In fact, Giles' statement that God "is not other than he reveals himself" is central to the eternal submission case. While not every aspect of the immanent Trinity is revealed in the economy, everything visible of the Trinity in the economy must have its counterpart in the immanent Trinity. Therefore, if Jesus is submissive to the Father in the economy of salvation, there must be *some* correspondence between this temporal reality and the eternal life of God. Yet Giles adamantly says there is no correspondence here.

This brings us to the third part of this section: can we legitimately separate the relationship of the Father and Son in the economy from their eternal relationship? Giles' argument is that this is what we must do, even though one sentence earlier he claims that the triune God is not other or different from the way he reveals himself in salvation history. To me, this is a critical point of error in the work of opponents of ESS. The idea that the relations between Father and Son are one way in the created world and another way in the eternal life of God means that the triune God *is* different immanently than he reveals himself economically. This is the very danger that Sanders alluded to when he wrote, "While nobody thinks there are two actual trinities involved in reality, the reduplicative phrasing puts two trinities into any sentence framed by economic and immanent."[33]

I am not arguing that what is said about Jesus and the Father during Jesus' first advent directly correlates with their eternal relationship *in every way* that we conceive of as humans. If that were the case, we might conclude that Jesus as Son was created by the Father, since human fathers beget sons, leading us into Arianism. Instead, the economic categories of Father and Son say *something*

---

31. Giles, *Jesus and Father*, 265.

32. This can be supported biblically from passages like Isa 55:9, Jer 23:23, and Rom 11:33.

33. Sanders, *Triune God*, 145.

A Theological Examination of Eternal Submission

about the eternal relationship between the two, but do not exhaust their eternal relationship. Additionally, as we saw in our discussion above, John 1:18 argues strongly that Jesus gives a "full account" of who God the Father is, both in reference to his unity with the Father and also in terms of his relationship with the Father.

By extension then, the Son's submission and obedience to the Father in the economy must have *some kind* of eternal correlation. To flatly say, as Giles does, that we cannot at some level read the authority and submission demonstrated in the economic relationship of the Father and Son back into their eternal divine life effectively creates two different trinities. This is highly problematic because it raises the question as to whether we can really and truly know God. But, again, John 1:18 affirms that Jesus makes the Father known, and by extension their eternal relationship.

The point must also be made that to limit Christ's submission to the Father to his humanity or to the economy of salvation divides the person of Christ into two parts: the incarnate Christ and the divine or eternal Christ. This brings one dangerously close to, if not guilty of, Nestorianism. Nestorius was the archbishop of Constantinople in the fifth century AD. He was concerned to preserve particularly the humanity of Christ amidst an atmosphere where Mary was titled "God-bearer" (*Theotokos*).[34]

> Jesus himself must have had a real humanity and have undergone growth, change and suffering and it was important to acknowledge this. Nestorius and Constantinople stood as the representatives of the Antiochene tradition in this debate. Not only were they concerned to affirm the humanity of Christ; they wanted to guard the *distinction* between his divinity and his humanity. They even listed words and deeds of Jesus that showed his divinity in action and those that showed his humanity.[35]

Nestorius' main opponent was Cyril of Alexandria, who argued, "Christians do not worship the man Jesus 'along with' (σύν) the Word, but rather 'one and the same Christ,' because his body cannot

---

34. Need, *Truly Divine*, 83.
35. Need, *Truly Divine*, 83.

be separated from the Word, as the former language suggests."[36] At the Council of Ephesus in 431 AD, Nestorius was condemned for his views, exiled, and died several years later. It was not until the Council of Chalcedon in 451 that the issue of the person of Christ and the relationship between his divine and human natures was more carefully laid out.

> As formulated at the Council of Chalcedon, what happened in the incarnation is that this divine hypostasis, or person took on a second nature without giving up or diminishing the first one. The incarnate Christ was therefore one divine hypostasis or person in two natures, one of which was divine and the other human. Cyril's claim that the two had become one was rejected; they were *united* in the person of Christ but not *merged*.[37]

The Chalcedon definition that laid out the relationship between the divine and human natures of Christ said he was:

> One and the same Christ, Son, Lord, Only-begotten, to be acknowledged in two natures, without confusion, without change, without division, without separation; the distinction of natures being in no way abolished because of the union, but rather the characteristic property of each nature being preserved, and concurring into one Person and one subsistence (ὑπόστασις), *not as if Christ were parted or divided into two persons*, but one and the same Son and only-begotten God, Word, Lord, Jesus Christ; even as the Prophets from the beginning spoke concerning him, and our Lord Jesus Christ instructed us, and the Creed of the Fathers has handed down to us.[38]

We notice that there are really two levels spoken of in regard to Christ here. He has two natures: human and divine. His divine nature is the same eternal divine nature he has always and will always possess. At the incarnation he takes to himself a human nature and forever unites it with his divine nature (cf. Phil 2:5–11). Christ,

---

36. Beeley, *Unity of Christ*, 260.
37. Morgan and Peterson, *Deity of Christ*, 181. Emphasis added.
38. Stevenson and Frend, *Creeds, Councils*, 405–6. Emphasis added.

A Theological Examination of Eternal Submission

therefore, has two natures that are united and without confusion, change, division, or separation. However, when we speak of the eternal person of the Son, there is only one. We cannot speak about a divine person of Christ and a human person of Christ. That is the Nestorian heresy condemned at Ephesus and Chalcedon.[39]

This factors into the present discussion in that as we examine the interplay between the economic and immanent aspects of God's triune life, it is important to understand that on the level of persons (and therefore relations, since relations are proper to the persons of the Trinity and not the divine essence), Jesus is *the same person* both eternally and in the incarnation. What is proper to the person of Christ does not change in the incarnation. What changes is that the divine nature or essence is joined with a human nature or essence. Therefore, if we place Christ's submission to the Father on the level of *person*, what is seen economically in the interactions between the person of the Father and the person of the Son must have its basis in eternity.

In this section I have argued against the idea that eternal submission collapses the economic Trinity into the immanent Trinity. There is only one Trinity, with immanent and economic aspects. We have seen that what we observe in the working of the economic Trinity in salvation history has its basis in the eternal life of God. Thus, if we see submission from the Son to the Father in his earthly life, it must reflect some eternal reality. We have also seen from the Nestorian debates of the fifth century AD that the person of Christ is the same in his incarnate life as he is in his eternal life. His *personhood* does not undergo change and is not affected by his taking on of humanity. The relations between Father and Son during the earthly life of Christ, therefore, must be a true and accurate representation of what occurs eternally.

---

39. Morgan and Peterson, *Deity of Christ*, 181.

Eternal Submission, Divine Simplicity, and the Divine Will

Perhaps one of the strongest arguments against ESS is that saying the Father possesses authority and the Son submits eternally does injustice to the orthodox representation of God as a simple being, not composed of parts, possessing one divine will. Millard Erickson writes, "The idea that there is one supreme will, that of the Father, and that the will of the Son and that of the Spirit are so separate from the will of the Father that they must eternally submit to that will does separate the persons considerably."[40] Kevin Giles agrees when he says, "The language of commanding and obeying implies that the parties involved each have their own will."[41] He continues:

> In relations between the divine Father, Son, and Spirit, perfect harmony prevails. They are one in mind and will. The idea that each divine person has his own will and the Son in particular is called to submit his will to that of the Father's will implies tritheism. To argue that the Son can do no other than obey, as the Sydney theologians do, means that he is not free and thus his actions are not obedience. He is a robot.[42]

Carl Trueman also views the one divine will through the lens of church history as an essential of orthodoxy. He writes:

> Nicene Trinitarianism involves a host of commitments—to divine simplicity as classically articulated by Gregory Nazianzus, to the unity of the divine will, to inseparable operations and, of course, to eternal generation. Repudiation or revision of any one or more of these involves a revision of the whole and thus ceases to be Nicene Trinitarianism.[43]

---

40. Erickson, *Who's Tampering?*, 218.
41. Giles, *Jesus and Father*, 203.
42. Giles, *Jesus and Father*, 203.
43. Trueman, "A Surrejoinder."

A Theological Examination of Eternal Submission

Goligher likewise states, "To speculate, suggest, or say, as some do, that there are three minds, three wills, and three powers with the Godhead is to move beyond orthodoxy (into neo-tritheism) and to verge on idolatry (since it posits a different God)."[44]

All of these voices argue that advocating for the eternal submission of the Son puts one outside the realm of orthodoxy by complicating the triune God beyond an eternal life of simplicity through the creation of multiple minds and wills in the Godhead. This essentially makes proponents of ESS no longer Trinitarian in their theology, but instead tritheists who worship three distinct gods and not one. In order to address this problem, I will first look at the concept of divine simplicity to see if it is ultimately incompatible with eternal submission. Second, I will address the question of whether the will of God is proper to the divine nature or instead to the persons. Finally, to conclude this section I will present several biblical texts that reinforce the idea that the will of God must be viewed both from God's essential unity and also from God's personal distinctions.

Erickson explains divine simplicity as meaning "that God's being does not involve any sort of metaphysical complexity whatsoever."[45] For Erickson, divine simplicity is related to unity:

> The other concern this doctrine addresses is the unity of the persons in the Trinity. The three persons are ultimately one. Thus, none of the various qualities that characterize God can be assigned as properties to one or the other of the members of the Trinity. Each person possesses all of these perfections.[46]

Grudem also points to the connection between God's unity and divine simplicity:

> The unity of God may be defined as follows: *God is not divided into parts, yet we see different attributes of God emphasized at different times.* This attribute of God has

---

44. Goligher, "Is it Okay?"
45. Erickson, *God the Father*, 213.
46. Erickson, *God the Father*, 230.

> also been called *God's simplicity*, using *simple* in the less common sense of "not complex" or "not composed of parts." But since the word *simple* today has the more common sense of "easy to understand" and "unintelligent or foolish," it is more helpful now to speak of God's "unity" rather than his "simplicity."⁴⁷

For both Erickson and Grudem, simplicity refers to the idea that God is a unified being. He is not composed of his attributes; in a very real sense he *is* his attributes.⁴⁸

If we operate with this understanding of the simplicity of the triune God, how does this impact the discussion of eternal submission? Is eternal submission incompatible with divine simplicity? The Son's submission to the Father, for many, implies a complexity that divides God into parts.

However, as K. Scott Oliphint argues, "Contrary to much of the literature, the doctrine of simplicity, in its best formulations, has never affirmed that God is some sort of being in which no distinctions are or could be made."⁴⁹ He continues:

> God's oneness is always and at the same time to be understood in terms of his threeness. Or, more specifically, the fact that God is not composed of parts in no way negates, subverts, or undermines the fact that the one God is three persons, and that the three are one; instead, the oneness *requires* the threeness, and vice versa. Important, therefore, to a biblical understanding of God is an affirmation of the doctrine of divine simplicity—an affirmation at the heart of any orthodox theology proper—that will also entail an affirmation of God as triune.⁵⁰

The point made above is that divine simplicity embraces both the oneness and threeness of God. Talking about authority and submission distinctions between Father and Son in the immanent Trinity, therefore, does not automatically jettison divine simplicity.

---

47. Grudem, *Systematic Theology*, 177–78.
48. Erickson, *God the Father*, 212.
49. Oliphint, "Simplicity, Triunity," 223.
50. Oliphint, "Simplicity, Triunity," 224.

A Theological Examination of Eternal Submission

Simplicity does not negate divine distinctions but makes those distinctions simply part of who God is as a simple being.[51] It is not impossible, therefore, to speak of God's unity or simplicity on the one hand, and also speak of personal distinctions like the eternal submission of the Son on the other.

Yet the question remains, does God possess one will or three? Orthodox Christianity has, from the fourth century AD onward, spoken of God as having one will. A large part of the Trinity debate of 2016 revolved around the issue of God's will and whether it left any room for eternal submission. Carl Trueman, in one recent article,[52] quotes Kyle Claunch to show that even proponents of ESS have recognized this move. Claunch writes:

> In order for the Son to submit *willingly* to the *will* of the Father, the two must possess distinct wills. This way of understanding the immanent Trinity does run counter to the pro-Nicene tradition, as well as the medieval, Reformation, and post-Reformation Reformed traditions that grew from it. According to traditional Trinitarian theology, the will is predicated of the one undivided essence so that there is only one divine will in the immanent Trinity.[53]

What Trueman does not say is that Claunch goes on to reject this three-willed view of God in his article and to defend eternal submission as compatible with one divine will.[54]

Claunch's argument is as follows: according to the Definition of Chalcedon, Christ possesses two natures, a human and a divine. "If will is associated with person, then Christ cannot possess a human will, but only a divine will because he is one divine person."[55]

---

51. Oliphint, "Simplicity, Triunity," 223. Oliphint says, "The distinctions that do reside in God, because they accrue to him essentially, are identical with him and thus are not parts of God, parts that would serve, in sum, to make up the whole of who he is. Oliphint, "Simplicity, Triunity," 223.
52. Trueman, "A Reply."
53. Claunch, "God Is the Head," 88.
54. Claunch, "God Is the Head," 88–92.
55. Claunch, "God Is the Head," 89.

Eternal Submission

The one will of God, therefore, must be proper to the divine nature. The persons of the Godhead are eternally differentiated by their processions (the Father generates the Son, the Father [and Son] spirate the Holy Spirit). "The eternal relationships of origin, which differentiate the three persons in the immanent being of God, entail a fixed and irreversible order in the one eternal and indivisible divine essence."[56] This coincides with divine simplicity in that "if the one essence of the Godhead subsists eternally as Father, Son, and Holy Spirit, then the one divine will subsists eternally as Father, Son, and Holy Spirit as well."[57] Claunch concludes:

> To say that the Son submits eternally to the will of the Father is, I propose, too strong precisely because it implies two distinct wills in relation to one another. It is preferable to say that, in the immanent Trinity, *the one eternal will of God is so ordered that it finds analogical expression in a created relationship of authority and submission: the incarnate Son submits to the will of his Father.*[58]

I agree with both Claunch and the tradition of the church throughout history that there must be one divine will. However, I would slightly modify Claunch's argument to say that the will of God has both *external* and *internal* facets, just as we saw with the issue of divine authority. When viewed from outside of the being of God, there is one absolute and unchanging will, just as God is one in essence. Yet on the level of personal distinctions, in the internal life of God there is a multiplicity to his will. Each of the persons of the Trinity contribute to or collaborate in the one divine will, but in diverse ways. This coincides, I believe, with Claunch's model of "thinking about the one divine will according to an eternal Trinitarian *taxis*,"[59] and fits nicely within the realm of Nicene Trinitarian orthodoxy.

Three biblical arguments give support to this hypothesis. First, Ephesians 1:11 refers to God the Father predestining

---

56. Claunch, "God Is the Head," 90.
57. Claunch, "God Is the Head," 91.
58. Claunch, "God Is the Head," 91.
59. Claunch, "God Is the Head," 92.

A Theological Examination of Eternal Submission

believers in Christ "according to His purpose who works all things after the counsel of His will." The term "counsel" (βουλή) is used at times in the LXX and NT to refer to *a collective decision* arrived at by a group.[60] The will of God in this verse is both individual and collective. The will spoken of in Ephesians 1:11 is primarily the Father's will, and the word occurs in the singular, emphasizing that there is one will. At the same time, the term βουλή implies a will or decision that is arrived at collectively. The will of God is referred to four times in these first eleven verses and is intertwined with both the working of the Father and the Son, who both work to accomplish the will of the Father.

The Greek word βουλή implied a multiplicity of thought toward a collective decision.[61] It is used in this sense in Acts 27:12 and 42, where, in both circumstances, a group comes to one decision or purpose.[62] Thus, the term envelops both the ideas of unity of mind and also diversity of thought. In Ephesians 1:11 there is ultimately one divine will (presented as the Father's will), but at the same time this will is something proper to the Father in a way that it is not proper to the Son. At the very least, this shows that the scriptural idea of God's will leaves room for both divine unity (simplicity) and personal distinctions in terms of the one divine will.

Second, a negative argument helps demonstrate the need for diversity as it relates to the one divine will. In Philippians 2:5–11, if one asserts that the Father, Son, and Spirit all possess one divine will, yet one denies meaningful distinctions in that will as it relates to the Trinitarian persons, the Son's taking the form of a man is ultimately not proper to the Son in a personal way; it is simply the outworking of the divine will. This is a sharp contrast to seeing the

---

60. For example: Gen 49:6; 1 Kgs 12:8, 14; Ps 1:1, 5; Lk 23:51; Acts 27:12, 42.

61. Schrenk, "βουλή," 633. Schrenk says, "βουλή denotes 'deliberation' and 'taking counsel' in all its stages and effects up to 'resolve' and 'decree.'" Schrenk, "βουλή," 633.

62. In Acts 27:12, the majority of the sailors decided to put to sea (ἔθεντο βουλὴν ἀναχθῆναι); in Acts 27:42, the soldier's plan was to kill the prisoners (ὧν δὲ στρατιωτῶν βουλὴ ἐγένετο ἵνα τοὺς δεσμώτας ἀποκτείνωσιν). Notice the singular form used for the counsel/purpose/plan arrived at by the group.

Eternal Submission

Son's preincarnate decision to humble himself as a *free* and *voluntary* expression of his divine love for humanity. Rather, it becomes the cold requirement of a Trinitarian person acting in a way that is bound by the collective thought.[63] Philippians 2 shows the need for the one divine will to have distinctive facets and applications appropriate to the level of the divine persons.

Third, Jesus' prayer to the Father in the Garden of Gethsemane[64] demonstrates distinctions in the divine will at the level of the Trinitarian persons. In his recent work, Michael J. Ovey has thoroughly examined the account of Jesus' prayer in Gethsemane.[65] He contests that the prayer shows "a real distinction of Persons," and "in some sense a plurality of wills."[66] He then offers three possibilities for handling the garden prayer of Christ when he says, "yet not as I will, but as Thou wilt" (Matt 26:39). The first possibility is that Jesus refers only to his natural human will. This option does not deal directly with the divine nature of Christ, and so must lead to two additional possibilities. The second option is that when Jesus speaks of the Father's will, he is referring to the one common divine will. The third possibility is that "Jesus' reference to wills is to be taken as a reference not to natural wills but to actualisations of will at the level of persons."[67]

In assessing these options, Ovey argues that seeing Jesus in this prayer as submitting his human will to the common divine triune will presents some major problems. For example, did the NT writers really conceive of a common divine nature, and would they have applied it to God the Father in this context?[68] In response, Ovey says seeing Jesus' prayer to the Father as really addressing

---

63. I would go further to argue that seeing one essential divine will without allowing for personal distinctions and expressions of that will ultimately leads to a form of modalism where there is really only one person operating within the Godhead.

64. Matt 26:39–46; Mark 14:32–42; Luke 22:39–46.

65. Ovey, *Your Will Be Done*, 105–14.

66. Ovey, *Your Will Be Done*, 107.

67. Ovey, *Your Will Be Done*, 108.

68. Ovey, *Your Will Be Done*, 110.

A Theological Examination of Eternal Submission

the triune God would mean Jesus *addressed himself* in prayer. He presents this reasoning as akin to that faced by Tertullian in responding to monarchianism,[69] and which leads one down the path to the dark side of Nestorianism.[70]

Ovey concludes that Jesus' reference to his will and the Father's will relates to the relations of God rather than to his divine nature.

> The reference to what each Person wills is to be taken within the context of personal relation rather than of the common nature/substance. As such, Jesus the Son in his unified coherent Person is praying for, and in the light of, the priority of his Father's will in their relationship . . . Far from being inconsistent with dyothelite theology, the eternal subordination of the Son fits well and preserves precisely that aspect, namely Jesus the Son as a unified and coherent Person, which is so important if dyothelitism is not to degenerate into Nestorianism.[71]

Ovey's work shows that there is a relational aspect to the will of God that must be viewed on the intra-Trinitarian level of persons, while at the same time maintaining the orthodox teaching of the church that there is one divine will. Differentiating between God's internal will on the relational level of divine persons, and God's external will on the level of divine unity, or being, reveals that eternal submission does not contradict the tradition of the church as it relates to simplicity and the divine will, but actually reinforces it. The will of God shows uniformity, and yet within that uniformity reveals a multifaceted distinctiveness in its application to the

---

69. Ovey, *Your Will Be Done*, 110.

70. Ovey, *Your Will Be Done*, 111. Ovey writes, "In what sense, if Jesus the Son wills one thing in his natural human will and another in his divine natural will, is there a genuine, unified, integrated Person? . . . Further, if we were to seek to eliminate this contradiction by simply saying his human will is swallowed up in his divine will, then this clearly raises serious questions about whether he retains all of his human nature in its full integrity." Ovey, *Your Will Be Done*, 111.

71. Ovey, *Your Will Be Done*, 112.

persons of Father and Son as they relate to one another in their eternal, immanent life.

Eternal Submission, Immutability, and Divine Freedom

Does eternal submission demand that Jesus is *necessarily* submissive based on the divine attribute of immutability? Is he eternally bound to obey the Father in the same way a slave is bound to obey their master because by nature he is unchanging? Does he have no choice but to submit to the will of his Father? This is the contention of Millard Erickson:

> The Son is *necessarily* subordinate to the Father. *He could not be otherwise.* Under any and all circumstances (or as it is sometimes put in philosophical discussions, "in all possible worlds"), the Father has authority over the Son and the Son is subordinate to the Father.[72]

Giles agrees: "If the Son *is*, and cannot be other than, the eternally submissive Son, surely He *is* the eternally subordinated Son. His person is defined by His unchanging subordering under the Father. If this is the case, then does it not imply ontological subordinationism?"[73]

Furthermore, if the Son is necessarily submissive to his father, what are the implications for divine freedom? D. Glenn Butner, Jr. addresses this question as follows:

> What would it mean for the Son to possess an identical will to the Father but to possess it in a way that could appropriately be called submission? J. Scott Horrell, an advocate of EFS, has clearly stated that we cannot posit that the Father and the Son would be free to differ from one another. I agree strongly with Horrell on this claim, as it would seem to be impossible for two omnipotent beings to will contrary things. If the Son is not free to differ

---

72. Erickson, *Who's Tampering?*, 171. Emphasis mine.
73. Giles, "Son of God," 17.

A Theological Examination of Eternal Submission

from the Father, then by EFS advocate Robert Letham's definition of submission . . . the Son cannot submit to the Father because such submission requires freedom."[74]

Freedom in the Godhead, Butner argues, cannot mean that the Son is free to differ from the Father in terms of will. So if the Son submits to the Father, he is acting in a way that is different than the Father, which implies a personal freedom that destroys the unity of the Godhead.

To respond to these problems raised against ESS, we will first look at divine immutability in conjunction with eternal submission and ask whether or not the two are compatible. This will require an examination of the claim that the eternal submission of the Son becomes *necessary* rather than *voluntary*. Second, we will look at freedom within the being of God as it relates to eternal submission, and assess the claim that divine freedom demands the Trinitarian persons cannot act independently of one another.

First, does it logically follow that if Christ submits to the Father eternally that his submission is also necessary? In other words, could he choose to do something other than submit? As we saw above, Erickson argues that the answer is a definitive "no."[75] He bases this on Grudem's statement, "These distinctions are essential to the very nature of God himself, and they could not be otherwise."[76] Grudem then contests that the relationships of authority and submission between the Father and the Son are essential to the nature of God. If Jesus the Son did not submit, God in his essence would be changing.

In response to this hypothetical situation, it seems that both Erickson and Grudem fail to acknowledge that Jesus as the eternally submissive Son does not submit under coercion or out of necessity, but voluntarily and freely. What Erickson focuses on is whether or not there is potential for the Son to be able to do other than submit. This takes a negative perspective on the question without examining the positive perspective. It is not that

74. Butner, Jr., "Eternal Functional Subordination," 147.
75. Erickson, *Who's Tampering?*, 171.
76. Grudem, *Systematic Theology*, 251.

Eternal Submission

Jesus *cannot* act but in obedience and submission to the Father; he volitionally *will not* act but in obedience and submission. While refusing to submit to the Father is in theory possible, the reality is that the Son would never choose anything but to submit. "He acts freely, not under compulsion. This tells us something vital about the Son and about God Himself."[77]

The answer to this argument may find a parallel in the question of whether or not God could sin. Erickson says in response to this hypothetical question that God "may have all of the abilities, the power, skill, and so on, to the acts that comprise sin, but doing them is not consistent with the kind of person he is."[78] Similarly, as the eternal divine Son, Jesus might have the potential ability to not submit to the Father's authority, but it would not be consistent with his eternal character. Therefore, an attempt to argue that Jesus is *necessarily* submissive to the Father would deny that Jesus *willingly* and *voluntarily* chose in eternity to become incarnate.

The question of divine freedom is intricately related to this issue. If Jesus is necessarily submissive to the Father, then the two differ from one another in that they are both independently free in a way that compromises divine unity.[79] Bruce Ware contests that this is only true, however, when viewed through the lens of liberaterian freedom.

> Butner's criticism only works if the freedom by which the Son is said to "freely obey" the Father is one in which he can equally obey or disobey the Father, i.e., the Son has libertarian freedom which requires the power of contrary choice. But I have argued elsewhere that libertarian freedom is a failed conception that neither explains why moral agents choose precisely what they do, nor does it accord with the strong sovereignty of God we see throughout the Scriptures.[80]

---

77. Letham, "Does the Son?," 14.
78. Erickson, *God the Father*, 179.
79. Butner, Jr., "Eternal Functional Subordination," 147.
80. Ware, "Knowing."

A Theological Examination of Eternal Submission

If liberaterian freedom does not align with a scriptural view of the freedom displayed between the persons of the triune God, what other option is there? Ware continues:

> If we adopt instead the conception of freedom in which our freedom consists in our unconstrained ability to do what we most want, or to act according to our highest inclination—sometimes referred to as a "freedom of inclination"—then this problem is removed. The Son's willing submission is his free and unconstrained expression of what he most wants to do when he receives the authoritative will of the Father, which is always, without exception, to embrace and carry out precisely what the Father gives him to do.[81]

A helpful way to rephrase Ware's response might be to say that rather than viewing the distinctive freedom of the Trinitarian persons as the ability to differ with one another we should view their freedom as the ability to supplement or complement one another. Divine freedom in this view would be proper to the nature of God, but it would also be employed distinctively by the divine persons in a complementary way so that the one divine freedom always manifests itself as the Father freely possessing authority to generate and send the Son, and the Son always freely submitting to that authority voluntarily.

Jesus the Son freely and voluntarily submits to his Father in their eternal, intra-Trinitarian relations. As we have seen in this section, there is no real problem saying Jesus submits to the Father on the level of divine relations while maintaining complete equality on the level of the divine nature or essence.[82] Submitting to the Father relationally does not necessitate subordination in essence because Jesus always *wants* to submit. He is never coerced, or forced, but is *voluntarily* the eternally submissive Son of God.

---

81. Ware, "Knowing."
82. Ware, "Equal in Essence," 14.

Eternal Submission

Eternal Submission and Inseparable Operations

Another objection to the eternal submission of the Son centers around the topic of inseparable operations. This doctrine affirms that the three persons that constitute the one God work in a way that is unified in all their actions in creation, redemption, and the accomplishment of future glory. In commenting on the work of Father, Son, and Spirit in creation, Goligher explains why the concept seemingly clashes with ESS:

> This one act of willing and doing occurred simply and immediately without any effort whatsoever on God's part—the inseparable operation of the persons: Father, Son (Word) and Spirit. In the Triune God the three "persons" think as one, will as one, rule as one and act as one, and God does so from the perfect rest of His eternal life. The persons' mutual indwelling and delight in each other is beyond our understanding. Their fellowship is unique and cannot be reproduced.[83]

Stephen Holmes, in an article on the inseparable operations of the Trinity, writes about the state of current scholarship on these operations:

> The ancient Latin slogan *opera trinitatis ad extra sunt indivisa* [the external works of the Trinity are indivisible] has not been universally popular recently. Indeed, it has been held up by some systematicians as a lapidary summary of everything Augustine and the Latins got wrong in their misappropriation of Greek Trinitarian theology. It, or at least the doctrine it summarizes, has fared better in Patristic scholarship, however; recent study on the fourth-century debates, let by Michel Barnes and Lewis Ayres, has stressed repeatedly and, to my mind, simply convincingly not just that pro-Nicene theologians universally held to the inseparability of divine operations, but that this principle was key to the logic of pro-Nicene theology, providing (alone with the related commitment

---

83. Goligher, "Is it Okay?"

to divine simplicity) one of its central bulwarks against the charge of tritheism.[84]

This demonstrates the recent chasm between theologians and church historians on the importance of the doctrine for Trinitarian studies. Systematic theologians are not necessarily convinced of its legitimacy while patristic scholars have argued its centrality to Nicene Trinitarianism.

This rift was evident in the Trinitarian debate in 2016, where Grudem and Ware were repeatedly charged with moving away from inseparable operations in terms of the inner life of the Trinity.[85] Ware's response to these accusations is illuminating for our discussion. First, Ware affirms inseparable operations at the level of God's oneness:

> Because each person of the Trinity possesses the identically same divine nature, each uses the same power and relies on the same knowledge and wisdom in conducting the various works that each does. So, there cannot be a separation or division in the work of the One God since each person participates fully in the One nature of God.[86]

At the same time, Ware argues, the inseparable operations of the one God are multifaceted at the relational level:

> But this does not preclude each person accessing, as it were, those qualities of the divine nature (e.g., power, knowledge, wisdom) distinctively yet harmoniously, according to their own hypostatic identities as Father, and as Son, and as the Holy Spirit, such that they bring to pass one unified result accomplishing the one work of God. In this way, the personal works of the Father, Son, and Spirit may be distinctive but never divided; each may focus on particular aspects of the divine work yet only together accomplish the one, harmonious, unified work of God.[87]

84. Holmes, "Trinitarian Action," 60.
85. Goligher, "A Letter"; Trueman, "A Surrejoinder"; Trueman, "A Reply."
86. Ware, "Knowing."
87. Ware, "Knowing."

Eternal Submission

Ware suggests that it is perfectly consistent to see the Trinity operating with one action while at the same time recognizing that each person contributes to that one action in distinctive, yet complementary, ways.

Creation is a good case in point. In the act of creation each of the persons of the Trinity are seen working together in unity toward one common goal, yet in diverse ways. Letham says on Trinitarian action in creation:

> The triadic manner of the earth's formation reflects who God, its Creator, is. He is a relational being. This is implicit from the very start. We notice distinctions among God, who created the heavens and earth (v. 1), the Spirit of God, who hovers over the face of the waters (v. 2), and the speech or word of God, issuing the fiat "Let there be light" (v. 3).[88]

The one act of creation, therefore, was performed in a multifaceted manner by each of the persons of the triune God acting in individualized ways that were unique to them. This is true not only for creation, but in regard to redemption, sanctification, and eschatological culmination. Indeed, this diversity in unity could be shown in all the works of God toward the created world. "This God, who created the universe, does not work in a monolithic way. His order is varied—it is threefold, but one. His work shows diversity in unity and unity in its diversity."[89]

At this point I would like to present three logical arguments as to why inseparable operations does not eliminate eternal submission as a divine possibility. First, to summarize Ware's argument above, speaking about God's work on the level of essence is very different from speaking about God's work on the level of person. Second, the inseparable operations of God must be viewed as relating to God's economic life rather than God's immanent life, or else we are thrust into confusion about the divine life of God. Third, if eternal submission goes against Nicene Trinitarianism in

---

88. Letham, *Holy Trinity*, 427.
89. Letham, *Holy Trinity*, 427.

A Theological Examination of Eternal Submission

the area of inseparable operations, by extension so must eternal generation. We now turn to examine each of these.

First, inseparable operations looks differently when viewed from the lens of the one divine nature than it does when viewed from the lens of the three divine persons. This was Ware's point in locating inseparable operations as applying to the essence or nature of God.[90] In regard to the triune God's divine oneness, the works of God must be viewed as inseparable. This reflects the teaching of Jesus in John 5:17 that united his working with the work of his Father. His audience understood this in terms of his equality with God the Father:

> But He answered them, "My Father is working until now, and I Myself am working." For this cause therefore the Jews were seeking all the more to kill Him, because He not only was breaking the Sabbath, but also was calling God His own Father, making Himself equal with God (John 5:17–18).

Yet the divine works look much differently when examined beginning with the threeness of God. In terms of divine distinctions, the works of the one God take on multiple dimensions in conjunction with the distinctive Trinitarian persons. Where one might conclude John 5:17–18 refers to the inseparable operations of the Father and Son as one God, the next verses stress the diversity of personal stance or relationship to that one inseparable operation:

> Jesus therefore answered and was saying to them, "Truly, truly, I say to you, the Son can do nothing of Himself, unless it is something He sees the Father doing; for whatever the Father does, these things the Son also does in like manner. For the Father loves the Son, and shows Him all things that He Himself is doing; and greater works than these will He show Him, that you may marvel" (John 5:19–20).

Within the work of the triune God in redemption, the Father and Son have distinctive parts that they play, or positions that they

90. Ware, "Knowing."

Eternal Submission

occupy. The inseparable operations of God, like God himself, are one operation with several dimensions, or angles, on that operation. The Father, Son, and Spirit each work "distinctively yet harmoniously"[91] to accomplish the one divine will.

Next, the inseparable operations of God should be seen as relating *exclusively* to God's economic life.[92] In other words, inseparable operations do not apply to the Trinity *ad intra* because by definition it is an *ad extra* feature. The very term "inseparable operations" implies the external working of the Trinity in the created universe. It is something done outside of the life of God as he eternally is. To apply this external category to an internal dimension of God's life is to confuse who God is with what he does.

This is exactly the confusion Stephen Holmes falls into when he writes about the relationship between inseparable operations and the Trinitarian relations of origin. Holmes attempts to examine the way that inseparable operations relates to eternal generation. Yet at the outset of his discussion of their relationship, he concedes that:

> The ancient slogan with which I began [*opera trinitatis ad extra sunt indivisia*] insists only that the external operations of the Trinity are inseparable, precisely because, I presume, there was an unwillingness to ask the speculative question concerning the eternal divine life.[93]

Holmes says further,

> Perhaps the wise theologian confesses all this to be true and then stops and refuses to speculate how any of this relates to the single power of the Trinity and the

---

91. Ware, "Knowing."

92. Sanders discusses this possibility when he says, "We could say that within the divine life itself there is no action leading to effects, because the life of God, being simple, is above the kind of distinctions implied in agency. Agency, on this view, would be something God has with respect to that which is not God. As for the life of God itself, we might describe its being as a very active Be-ing." Sanders, however, opts for the traditional view of speaking of internal works as opposed to external works. Sanders, *Triune God*, 130–33.

93. Holmes, "Trinitarian Action," 67.

A Theological Examination of Eternal Submission

inseparability of the divine operations; certainly this seems to have been the general Patristic answer.[94]

Holmes, in spite of acknowledging the important distinction between God's works and God's inner life, goes on to speculate about how these two dimensions of who God is and what he does might correlate. What is true of the unified works of God and the eternal divine processions is also true about the unified works of God as it relates to the eternal submission of the Son. Inseparable operations is an *ad extra* category which applies to God's actions outside of himself. To posit how this category might affect God *ad intra* not only moves into the speculative world, as Holmes suggests, but crosses categories to impose something that God *does* backward upon who God *is* in his eternal divine life.

The third logical argument is that if eternal submission cannot be true because of the inseparable operations of the Trinity, then by comparison eternal generation cannot be true as well. The reason for this is simple. If there is one divine work that applies not only to the external works of God in the created world but also back into the eternal life of God, then the eternal generation of the Son and the eternal spiration of the Spirit must also be one divine act.[95] This cannot be the case for multiple reasons.

If eternal generation is one eternal and divine *act*, then there is ultimately only one divine person. The Father has to *do* something to generate the Son, and in the same action, the Son who is generated works with the Father to spirate the Spirit. Holmes is clear this eternal action is simple, single, and unrepeatable.[96] However, that it is an action at all implies it is something done *outside of oneself*. If it is something the Father *does*, then there must be an object or objects acted upon—in this case, the Son and the Spirit. This stands in contrast to viewing generation and spiration as proper to the *relations* between the persons, which implies an order or *taxis* to

---

94. Holmes, "Trinitarian Action," 67–68.

95. This is precisely what Holmes argues. Holmes, "Trinitarian Action," 71. Holmes speaks of this event or act as "the one eternal divine operation," and as equivalent with "the divine life."

96. Holmes, "Trinitarian Action," 71.

Eternal Submission

the three persons in terms of their internal authority. Additionally, if eternal generation is a divine *act*, the implication is that there was something *prior to* or *apart from* that act. One can deny all day long that generation implies inferiority among the divine persons, but if one speaks of an *event* as initiating generation and spiration there is one kind of God *before* this event and a different God *after*.

If eternal generation does not run along the same categorical lines as inseparable operations as one relates to the divine nature and one to divine personhood, it is inconsistent to say that eternal generation does not contradict inseparable operations but eternal submission does. Both eternal generation and eternal submission relate directly to the persons of the Godhead and not directly to the divine essence. Therefore, opponents of ESS who accuse it of being incompatible with God's inseparable operations must be willing to either say eternal generation is a divine action/event, or recognize that generation and inseparable operations relate to two different categories: the *internal* life of God and the *external* works of God.

In sum, the inseparable operations of God in his unity do not relate in the same way to God in his intra-Trinitarian life. To accuse proponents of the eternal submission of the Son as being inconsistent with the inseparable operations of the triune God fails to distinguish between God's works in relation to the created world outside himself and the intra-personal relations within the eternal life of God.

Eternal Submission and Eternal Generation

The final theological area of defense for ESS comes in the connection between the eternal submission of the Son and the eternal generation of the Son. It has become very popular to espouse the second of these doctrines while disparaging the first. In this section, I want to first seek to describe (as best as humanly possible) eternal generation. Second, I want to briefly comment on the μονογενής controversy in recent years as it relates to eternal generation. Third, I want to present and critique Kevin Giles' discussion of the relationship between eternal generation and eternal

A Theological Examination of Eternal Submission

submission. Finally, I will offer several reasons why eternal generation and eternal submission should be viewed not only as compatible but truly as complementary doctrines.

Eternal generation is a doctrine proper to the relationship between the persons of the Godhead whereby the Father generates the Son eternally. The most common form of a statement concerning eternal generation comes from the Creed of Constantinople in 381 AD:

> We believe in one God the Father almighty, maker of heaven and earth, of all things visible and invisible; And in one Lord Jesus Christ, the only begotten Son of God, begotten from the Father before all ages, light from light, true God from true God, begotten not made, of one substance with the Father, through Whom all things came into existence.[97]

From this statement, we see that the Son is begotten from the Father before creation, and at the same time is not different from the Father in nature (he is "of one substance with the Father"). He is begotten, not made, which was stated as such to preserve his unity with the Father in essence, while allowing for personal distinction.

But what does the term "begotten" entail? Are we to think of this begetting in similar terms as a human father begetting a son? The work of Robert Letham is valuable at this juncture. In a recent article he offers six "basic entailments" of eternal generation.[98] They are:

1. Eternal generation is a divine mystery, beyond our human capacity for understanding.

2. Eternal generation cannot be compared with human generation, except that the generator and the one generated possess the same nature.

3. Eternal generation does not leave any room for the Son to be a created being in any way.

---

97. Stevenson and Frend, *Creeds, Councils*, 133.
98. Letham, "Eternal Generation," 119–21.

Eternal Submission

4. Eternal generation reveals the distinction in person between Father and Son while allowing for their essential unity.

5. Eternal generation "highlights an irreversible hypostatic order . . . Thus, the Father sends the Son, the Spirit proceeds from the Father, and the Spirit is sent by the Son—never the reverse."

6. Eternal generation binds together our understanding of the Trinity. It helps us understand eternal relationship between the three persons that constitute the one eternal God.[99]

These statements are helpful in understanding the scope of what eternal generation entails. However, in recent years, the doctrine of eternal generation has come under heavy criticism. Erickson has said of the doctrine:

> It must be acknowledged that for many persons today, the doctrine does not seem to make much sense. Just what does it mean to say that the Father eternally generates the Son, yet that the Son is not therefore inferior to the Father? How can the Father be the basis of the Son's being but without this constituting some species of creation of the latter by the former?[100]

Bruce Ware likewise has commented:

> The conceptions of both the "eternal begetting of the Son" and "eternal procession of the Spirit" seem to me highly speculative and not grounded in biblical teaching. Both the Son as only-begotten and the Spirit as proceeding from the Father (and the Son) refer, in my judgment, to the historical realities of the incarnation and Pentecost, respectively.[101]

These two criticisms show that areas of concern related to eternal generation are the logical feasibility of the doctrine as well as its biblical support.

99. Letham, "Eternal Generation," 119–21.
100. Erickson, *Who's Tampering?* 182.
101. Ware, *Father, Son*, 162, n. 2.

A Theological Examination of Eternal Submission

One reason eternal generation has come under attack has been its connection with the biblical term "only begotten" (μονογενὴς) and recent scholarship on the term. Many modern biblical scholars from the 1990s onward believed that μονογενὴς in Greek thought had less to do with begetting and more to do with uniqueness and being "one of a kind." Grudem in particular has argued in this way.

> For many years [μονογενὴς] was thought to be derived from two Greek terms: *mono*, meaning "only," and *gennaō*, meaning "beget" or "bear." Even the recent version of the Nicene Creed understands it that way, since the explanatory phrases "*begotten* of the Father before all worlds" and "*begotten*, not made" both use the verb *gennaō* (beget) to explain *monogenēs*. But linguistic study in the twentieth century has shown that the second half of the word is not closely related to the verb *gennaō* (beget, bear), but rather to the term *genos* (class, kind). Thus the word means rather the "one-of-a-kind" Son or the "unique" Son.[102]

Although defending eternal generation as an important doctrine, Giles takes a similar view of μονογενὴς.[103] Citing the work of Dale Moody, who examined the term in a 1950s study, Giles concludes:

> His [Moody's] essay tells us that this doctrine is not supported by appeal to the word *monogenēs*, and no text in the Old or New Testaments explicitly speaks of the "eternal" begetting or generation of the Son. From the perspective of a historical and critical reading of the Scriptures, his conclusions, I believe, cannot be disputed. They have gained wide scholarly support and should be accepted as conclusive.[104]

Thus, for both Grudem and Giles (at least until recently; Grudem now has changed his position[105]) the term had no connection to

---

102. Grudem, *Systematic Theology*, 1233.
103. Giles, *Eternal Generation*, 66.
104. Giles, *Eternal Generation*, 66.
105. Giles, *Rise and Fall*, 45–46.

Eternal Submission

the doctrine of eternal generation. The lack of biblical connection, particularly with regard to μονογενὴς, caused Grudem to avoid use of eternal generation in his systematic theology.

However, in just the past two years there has been renewed support for eternal generation within evangelicalism, led by key patristic and Trinitarian scholars who have argued convincingly for the legitimacy of eternal generation. This renewed support, interestingly, has risen from both those who deny ESS and those who affirm it. Giles has argued strongly for eternal generation while denying eternal submission.[106] Goligher and Trueman likewise see the necessity of the doctrine.[107] In the recent work edited by Bruce Ware and John Starke, several essays present eternal generation as an important aspect of Trinitarian discussion. Fred Sanders notes this important point in a review of the book:

> If this book is packaged as an Eternal Functional Subordination sandwich, it's the meat between the Grudem and Ware bread slices that's the big surprise. Like a Narnian stable or a Tardis, this book is considerably bigger on the inside than on the outside. What's eternal, and essential to the divine being, is Sonship, which means eternal generation and the filial generatedness that it entails. Is the obedience of the Son's will to the Father's commanding authority also eternal? That seems to me to be a fairly small question, and also one that needs an answer so nuanced it's practically a change of subject.[108]

Support for the doctrine of eternal generation also comes from new studies reexamining the μονογενὴς controversy. The work of Lee Irons has challenged popular scholarship concerning the validity and definitiveness of claiming the term means "unique" or "one of a kind."[109] Irons says of his work, "I argue that while it

---

106. Giles, *Eternal Generation*. Interestingly, Giles affirms translating μονογενὴς as "unique/one of a kind" rather than "only begotten."

107. Goligher, "Is it Okay?"; Trueman, "Once More."

108. Sanders, "Things Eternal."

109. Irons, "Let's Go Back." See also Iron's chapter in Sanders and Swain, *Retrieving Eternal Generation*.

A Theological Examination of Eternal Submission

is used with the meaning 'unique' in certain contexts, the most basic meaning is 'only begotten' in extra-biblical Greek. I further believe that 'only begotten' is the best rendering of the word in the five Johannine passages."[110] Additionally, a very recent collection of essays entitled *Retrieving Eternal Generation* has been compiled to give biblical, theological, historical, and philosophical weight to the legitimacy of the doctrine.[111]

Kevin Giles has an entire book devoted to the important topic of eternal generation.[112] In it he outlines the importance of the doctrine for Trinitarian studies. What is significant for our discussion is that Giles refuses to see any connection between eternal generation and submission. He is adamant that generation does not necessitate the eternal subordination of the Son to the Father.[113] His arguments, summarized at the end of the chapter, are:

1. Eternal generation does not denote a change in God's being.

2. Eternal generation is not like human generation, except in that human fathers and sons share the same nature, as do the divine persons.

3. Eternal generation "is not to be understood in terms of temporal, contingent causation or as human begetting in the created order." It is an act that takes place within the life of God.

4. Eternal generation is the basis for the Son's true deity.

5. Eternal generation differentiates Father and Son in terms of relations, not essence.[114]

While Giles is right to defend the eternal generation of the Son, and right to guard against equating eternal generation with *ontological* subordination, he is wrong to advocate that generation

---

110. Irons, "Μονογενής."
111. Sanders and Swain, *Retrieving Eternal Generation*.
112. Giles, *Eternal Generation*.
113. Giles, *Eternal Generation*, 205–19. Giles does not distinguish in this chapter between those who subordinate the Son ontologically and those who see the Son's subordination in terms of relations or roles.
114. Giles, *Eternal Generation*, 218–19.

Eternal Submission

and *relational* submission are not connected. In the next several paragraphs I want to first point out some factors that show eternal generation and voluntary submission to be complementary, not mutually exclusive. Second, I will present the inconsistency in Giles' approach of accepting eternal generation but rejecting eternal submission.

Giles understands eternal generation as a "divine act *ad intra*."[115] This is largely based off his reading of Thomas Aquinas, who "spoke explicitly of the Son's begetting and the Spirit's 'spiration' as divine acts *ad intra*, to be contrasted with divine acts *ad extra*."[116] Yet, as I have argued above, this terminology superimposes an economic Trinitarian activity (God's "doing" or actions) to the internal, relational life of God.[117] Perhaps it would be better not to talk about God's actions *ad intra*, but rather to take eternal generation to apply solely to the *relations* of the Trinitarian persons apart from *actions*.[118] This would mean eternal generation is not properly a divine act but instead a divine relationship. The Father is eternal generator, the Son eternally generated, and this would describe their fundamental relationship to one another.[119]

The Father as generator and the Son as generated implies an irreducible order, or *taxis*, between these persons. Letham agrees:

> There is an order (*taxis*) among [the Trinitarian persons]. This is not an order of rank, as the Arians and Eunomians argued, in which the three are arranged in some form of hierarchy. It is more akin to a suitable disposition, a well-arranged constitution . . . Thus, the Father begets

---

115. Giles, *Eternal Generation*, 219.

116. Giles, *Eternal Generation*, 217.

117. Another way to phrase this would be to ask the question, "What Trinitarian actions occur in the immanent Trinity?" Action implies something that is external to oneself. Eternal generation, on the other hand, is an internal reality, which is why I wonder if is not better to speak of as a relation rather than an action.

118. See Sanders, *Triune God*, 130–33 for a discussion of the legitimacy of God's internal works. While Sanders makes a case for viewing God's actions as only external, he opts for a more traditional approach.

119. This seems to be what Giles is saying in his fifth point above.

A Theological Examination of Eternal Submission

the Son and spirates the Spirit, the Son is begotten, and so on. In turn, the Father sends the Son, and the Father and the Son send the Spirit. These relations are not reversible, although the three have a mutuality since they are all equal, and are each—as well as together—the whole God.[120]

The two persons, therefore, do not relate to each other in the same way. It is an asymmetrical relation. The Father is not generated by the Son. The Father in the equation of eternal generation is seen as the base or starting point of the relations. The Son is spoken of in terms of his relationship with the Father. The Father eternally begets (generates) the Son. In each statement, the Father is the subject, with the Son being the recipient of the Father's actions. D. A. Carson agrees when he says,

> If there is a certain *taxis* in the Trinity, then in some highly qualified ways it may not be inappropriate to speak of the obedience and subordination of the Son even while we robustly insist that he is in no way inferior to his Father in essence, glory, power, majesty, perfections, and holiness, which of course is what the eternal generation of the Son is designed to protect while still depicting him as the *Son* of God.[121]

Within the doctrine of eternal generation, then, is inextricably bound the primacy (authority) of the person of the Father, and the reception of that authority by the Son. The Father's authority in the internal life of God is demonstrated by his eternally generating the Son, and the Son's passive submission is demonstrated in his being generated by the Father.

There is also an inconsistency in Giles' approach that should be pointed out here. He repeatedly refuses to allow any submission

---

120. Letham, *Holy Trinity*, 491.

121. Carson, "John 5:26," 96. Carson goes on to say, "Indeed, John 5:26 celebrates that the Son has the same 'life in himself' as the Father, which implicitly denies dependence and contingency, at least in the immanent Trinity, while the same verse in making such 'life in himself' an eternal grand surely bespeaks some kind of dependence, however carefully we wish to guard the expression." Carson, "John 5:26," 96.

into the internal life of God because "historical revelation never captures fully the divine reality."[122] While he is adamant about this point in terms of the ESS discussion, he seems much looser when it comes to eternal generation. "The eternal begetting of the Son cannot be likened to human generation, except on one matter: like produces like, and thus fathers and their offspring are of the same nature."[123]

What makes this one matter an exception to Giles' rule? Given that he loosely quotes the Nicene Creed here, it is probable that, for Giles, the Creed allows for the exception. Giles inconsistently allows for an aspect of human generation to inform our understanding of divine generation while refusing to consider the same in terms of human submission and obedience informing our understanding of divine submission.[124] The cause of this appears to be that eternal generation is mentioned in the Nicene Creed, while eternal submission is not. But should we be satisfied with that reasoning? If a human analogy is allowed for the relationship of eternal generation, why should a human analogy not be allowed in terms of eternal submission?

To summarize the discussion in this section, eternal generation and eternal submission are inseparably related. The Father's role in generating the Son and the Son's role in being generated reveal not only the irreducible order between the two divine persons, but further the primacy of the Father in generating and the receptive/submissive role of the Son in being generated. Eternal generation is proper to the relations between the Trinitarian persons and not to the divine nature.

Fred Sanders has brilliantly said,

> There is, in the relations of origin of the triune God, an irreversible taxis to which the obedience of the incarnate Christ corresponds in human form. It's an eternal procession that reaches its strangely logical final conclusion

---

122. Giles, *Jesus and Father*, 265.

123. Giles, *Eternal Generation*, 219.

124. The most likely reason for this is that ESS has no explicit creedal support as does eternal generation.

A Theological Examination of Eternal Submission

in the sending of the Son. As for his submission to the Father, I don't know what they call it in the happy land of the Trinity, but when it lives among us it is rightly named obedience.[125]

I would offer that in these areas both the terms "generation" and "submission" fall short of their eternal truths. Imperfect as they are, however, these terms are the best we have to denote important relational distinctions among the three persons that constitute the one eternal God.

Summary of Theological Examination

This chapter has argued for the legitimacy of eternal submission in six different (but intricately related) ways. Much of the discussion centers around a confusion between the discussions of, on one hand, God's unity, his oneness, his essence; and on the other hand, God's personhood, his relationality, his distinctions and diversity. There is, then, a sense in which we can talk about the authority, will, and operations of the triune God in both an absolute sense relating to God's unity, and in a relative sense relating to God's diversity.

These two alternate aspects of speaking about God relate to the way we view him. If we view God from the outside, that is, his external actions and stance toward the created world, we generally are met with the absolute oneness of God. If we consider God as he is internally, within his own intra-personal life (i.e., the way the distinct persons relate to one another), we are met with the threeness of God. Opposition to eternal submission has come largely when categories are crossed and the doctrine is made to stand in the arena of God's oneness. When located in its proper arena of the threeness of God, however, the doctrine of eternal submission finds fertile biblical and theological soil in which to take root.

---

125. Sanders, "Things Eternal." While Sanders was not arguing in support of eternal submission here, his comments leave the door open for correlation between Christ's human obedience to the Father and some kind of eternal corollary.

Chapter 6

The Implications of Eternal Submission

This paper has argued that Jesus the Son of God is eternally submissive to his Father in their intra-Trinitarian relationship with one another. Eternal submission applies not to the being or nature of God, but to the relations and personal inter-workings among the Trinitarian persons. In other words, Jesus is not ontologically subordinate in any way, being fully God and equally possessing full deity along with the Father and the Holy Spirit. At the same time, Jesus always chooses to submit willingly to his Father within the happy land of the Trinity,[1] where only the three reside in perfection forever. He is not *necessarily* submissive, as if the Father demands this submission from him, but is voluntarily so. Submission thus relates to the threeness of God, and not to his oneness.[2] There are a considerable number of implications of this study for other areas of theology.

---

1. A term used by Fred Sanders in *Deep Things*, 67–88.
2. Ware, *Father, Son,* 72.

The Implications of Eternal Submission
For Trinitarian Theology

In regard to Trinitarianism, the eternal submission of the Son demands a more carefully nuanced expression of information about the triune God. Much of the present debate over ESS has consisted of scholars talking past one another because they are crossing the distinctive categories of divine essence and divine persons, applying what is proper to the essence to personhood, or vice versa. Aditionally, the categories of the economic and the immanent Trinity have not been carefully correlated and need a reexamination. I want to briefly expand on both these areas.

First, it is essential to use Trinitarian terminology in a consistent manner. Some Trinitarian terms apply exclusively to God's unity (essence, nature) and others to God's diversity (person, relations). There are some terms that could and perhaps should be applied in both of the above areas (authority, will, operations). Still others (generation, submission) are proper only to divine relations. The twin perspectives of God's unity and diversity should be viewed as parallel rails on a railroad track: they are independent of one another and should be discussed as such. Yet both are necessary for the one God in three persons to be who he is and do what he does.

To demand that eternal submission necessitates ontological subordination crosses categories. To say that the one divine authority of God, demonstrated outside of the life of God, does not allow for submission in the internal life of God, crosses categories. To view the one essential divine will as shared absolutely without diversity of participation in and application of that will crosses categories and creates a modalistic god. To say that the natural (essential) simplicity and immutability of God should apply on the level of persons crosses categories. To view eternal generation as properly relational, while refusing to allow the possibility of the same in the area of submission is inconsistent.

Second, further consideration should be given to the relationship between the immanent and economic aspects of the Trinity. I have argued above that regulating the Son's submission to the Father in the created world alone too sharply divides the immanent and economic Trinity. For Jesus to accurately reveal the Father, his incarnate relationship with the Father must not be wholly different from their eternal relationship.

Furthermore, even the terminology of "economic" and "immanent," although prevalent in scholarship today, can be misleading and detrimental to a consistent application of other Trinitarian terminology.[3] Perhaps it would be better to speak of God's internal relations as compared with his external functions. This distinction could be helpful in comparing and contrasting Trinitarian terms that can apply to both the unity of God and his diversity. For example, in relation to the created world (externally), God possesses one absolute will exhibited absolutely. In terms of his inner life, however, there are multiple facets to that one will as it is applied to the three persons distinctively in relation with one another. The terminology of economic and immanent Trinity, therefore, requires more careful nuance and explanation by contemporary scholars.

For Theological Anthropology

What are the implications of the eternal submission of the Son for humanity and human relationships? It is popular today to argue that there are no legitimate implications even if it can be shown that ESS has biblical and theological ground on which to stand.[4]

---

3. For example, the implicit dichotomy of the Trinity into two trinities, as Fred Sanders points out. Sanders, *Triune God*, 145. Also, this speaking tends toward viewing the Trinity as falling into one of these categories, when in reality, the immanent Trinity never changes or ceases to function, even during the earthly life of Christ.

4. Goligher says, "To say, suggest, or speculate that God's life in heaven sets a social agenda for humans is to bring God down to our level. The eternal life of God as He is in Himself is incomprehensible to us and impossible to reproduce except by analogy. The life of the Three-in-One cannot be replicated by creatures. To use the intra-Trinitarian relations as a social model is neither biblical nor orthodox." Goligher, "Is it Okay?" Sanders writes, "Connecting Trinity to gender roles is a dangerously distracting pedagogical gambit. It bundles the doctrine of God with another set of commitments. To the extent that the doctrine of the triune God already seemed distant and abstract, this

The Implications of Eternal Submission

I want to summarize here why I believe there are implications for humanity. First, humanity is created in the image of God, and as such reflects in limited (and, because of sin, imperfect) and finite ways the perfect character of the infinite God.[5] Second, given the *imago Dei*, patterns of authority and submission between human persons must be in some way reflective of the relations of the divine persons. Third, we should be extremely cautious in making explicit or over-emphasizing what Scripture only hints at: that authority and submission between men and women in the church and home is analogous to the eternal life of God. Fourth, authority and submission relationships between human persons do have the potential to image God, and it is not restricted to male-female relations. We will briefly examine each of these.

First, it is important to view eternal submission within the context of theological anthropology in general. Human beings have been created uniquely in the image of God. No other part of the created order can claim this privileged position. Theologians today view the *imago Dei* as encompassing a number of facets.[6] Human beings have intellect, emotion, and will, which reflect those same characteristics within the life of God. Human beings are given authority to rule over the created order; this is a reflection

---

bundling strategy becomes the central importance of Trinitarianism. I know students who learned nothing from Trinity lectures except that the doctrine does or does not support egalitarianism or complementarianism. Of course I can blame the students for selective listening and motivated non-retention. But it also makes me think that including this topic in Trinity lectures is a very bad idea. Catechesis is too short for these dalliances, and the Trinity is too busy to serve as the transcendent ground of gender." Sanders, "18 Theses."

5. I have in mind not only the intellect, emotion, and will traditionally associated with God's image in humanity, but also the attributes of God that have been imprinted on humanity (such as love, justice, etc.), and the relational element of the Trinitarian persons living in perfect unity.

6. Anthony A. Hoekema says of these aspects, "The image of God in man must therefore be seen as involving both the structure of man (his gifts, capacities, and endowments) and the functioning of man (his actions, his relationships to God and to others, and the way he uses his gifts). To stress either of these at the expense of the other is to be one-sided." Hoekema, *Created*, 73. I would add that this beautifully mirrors both the oneness and threeness of God that has been discussed in this thesis.

Eternal Submission

of God's ultimate authority. Human beings also possess a relational or social element (God created them male and female), reflecting the three persons within God's one eternal life. The connection is not explicitly to gender here; human genders do not necessitate divine genders between the persons. But broadly we can say that just as there are relational distinctions between God the Father, the Son, and the Holy Spirit, so there are relational distinctions between men and women (and by extension, each individual to other individuals).

Second, if it is accepted that part of what it means to be created in God's image entails relationality, it follows that our relationships do have some correspondences to the internal life of God.[7] The argument that we should not read into the internal life of God *some aspects of* human relations fails to do justice to the *imago Dei*. God intended humanity to learn something about himself in Trinity through inter-personal relationships. Yet these reflections of God's relationality have been distorted by sin, and so we cannot look exclusively or uncritically at our human relationships as a guide for understanding Trinitarian relations. Here the word of God is the best guard against an unrestrained "social Trinitarianism" that imposes human categories on God's inner life. Since we see in the life of Jesus authority and submission demonstrated between the Father and Son, we can rightly agree with Karl Barth when he said, "As we look at Jesus Christ we cannot avoid the astounding conclusion of a divine obedience."[8]

Third, while we can make some connections between human and divine relationships, we should be extremely cautious in making explicit or over-emphasizing what Scripture only alludes to: that authority and submission between men and women in the church and home is analogous to the eternal life of God. While I have argued this is the best interpretation of 1 Corinthians 11:3,

---

7. As discussed earlier, this is because the economic and immanent Trinity are not two different trinities. There is consistency within the triune God in both his stance toward creation and apart from creation. Everything demonstrated in the economic Trinity must have a true and consistent corollary within the immanent Trinity.

8. Barth, *Church Dogmatics*, 202.

The Implications of Eternal Submission

it is not the primary scriptural reasoning given for male-female relational ordering, either in the home or in the church.[9] In the home, wives submit to husbands as the church submits to Christ (Eph 5:22–24), not as the Son submits to the Father. In the church, women are not permitted to teach or exercise authority over men because Adam was created first, and then Eve later (1 Tim 2:12–14), not because the Son submits to the Father. It is important to use the pictures that we are *clearly* given in the NT rather than focusing on pictures coming from difficult texts (like 1 Cor 11:3). Thus, extreme caution should be taken when employing Trinitarian relational realities as evidence for human role ordering.[10]

While we should be very hesitant to over-emphasize the intra-Trinitarian relationship between Father and Son to submission in human relationships, the alternate extreme of not mentioning it at all should be avoided as well. It is important to teach human persons in submissive roles that their submission is not viewed from the divine perspective as weakness, or some form of divine retribution, but as a divine characteristic. This is because within the intra-Trinitarian life of God, Jesus the Son is eternally disposed toward doing his Father's will. He delights to do his Father's will

---

9. First Cor 11:3 is a difficult text because it may be saying that men categorically possess an authority over women categorically, as Christ over men categorically, and the Father over Christ. In our culture this statement seems radically sexist and patriarchal. However, 1 Tim 2:8–15 might inform our reading of 1 Cor 11:3 in that the reason implied for men's position of authority over women might be related to their created order. This would not necessarily demand a parallel of created order between Father and Son, since the statements are not listed in a sequence, and the reason for their ordering is not made explicit. The term "head" then would be closer to "source" in that Christ created man, man was created first and then woman (and women physically created from men), and God the Father eternally generates Christ. First Cor 11:3 may also be referring to the marital relationship.

10. By extreme caution, I am really focusing on the way this is presented in teaching settings. Negatively stated, it is my conviction that the relationship between Trinitarian authority and submission and human should never become an imperative for the Christian life, because the NT does not use it that way. Positively stated, submissive human parties should be encouraged that their submission reflects a divine characteristic, particularly displayed in the life of the Son (1 Pet 2:18–25).

from eternity. Contrary to what Giles believes, it is in this sense that "voluntary subordination is godlike."[11] Teaching that submission is divine can be done without ever mentioning ESS by focusing on the submissive character of Christ in his earthly life, for his humanity and deity are inseparably linked in the incarnation.

In 1 Peter 2:18–25, Peter does exactly this by showing that Christ's suffering at the hands of the Jewish leaders was a faithful act of patient endurance. Christ's willing subjection to the Jewish authorities, ultimately leading to death on a cross, revealed in the end not weakness, but strength as he "kept entrusting *Himself* to Him who judges righteously" (1 Pet 2:23). He then encourages his readers to suffer well in like manner. Christ's willful submission to human authorities does not equate to eternal submission. However, his obedience to the Father in going to the cross means that his submission to human authorities was performed in light of that ultimate eternal submission. Eternal submission on the part of the Son, then, is the basis for human submission to authority that is performed voluntarily in love.[12]

Devotionally, then, the doctrine of eternal submission should not be used as a rod of enforcement by authoritarian parties seeking to make sure those subject to them get in line and obey their desires. Practically, pastors should avoid using the doctrine in the form of a negative argument like, "If you (submissive party) are not obeying your (authoritarian party), you are distorting the Trinitarian picture of the Son submitting to his Father." That kind of reasoning is unhelpful in doing anything but generating guilt and encouraging totalitarianism.

Rather, the doctrine of eternal submission can be used as positive encouragement and motivation for submissive persons.

---

11. Giles, *Trinity & Subordinationism*, 18. Giles uses this phrase to speak of the voluntary subordination of the Son to the Father during his incarnation only, denying that the Son submit eternally. By way of contrast, I use the phrase with the intended meaning that the Son eternally submits to the Father and does so voluntarily.

12. Christ's economic submission here demonstrates an eternal submission because of the consistency between the economic and immanent Trinity. Economic submission is based on eternal submission.

The Implications of Eternal Submission

For example, within the husband-wife relationship, the two are called "one flesh"[13] (Gen 2:24), and yet they are distinct persons. Wives are called to submit to their husbands, showing a divine mandate on the ordering of those personal relationships. This is reflective of the one God who eternally exists in three persons, with an internal ordering of those personal relationships. When a wife submits to a husband willingly and voluntarily, not because of his coercion, she is imaging God the Son in a very particular way. This leads us into the final point.

Fourth, human authoritarian and submissive relationships have the potential to image God in his inner life. Redeemed persons in authoritarian positions can follow the example of the Father, who does not abuse his power and authority, but always wields authority in love. Redeemed persons in submissive positions can follow the example of the Son, who receives the commands of the Father and delights to do his will. He voluntarily submits and obeys. This is not limited to male-female relationships but should be viewed in terms of all relationships that contain elements of authority and submission. In the NT, the most common of these relationships given are the husband-wife, parent-child, and master-slave. Each has application in our present context (master-slave being congruent to employer-employee).[14] It would be highly valuable to think through applications of Christ's eternal submission to his Father to each of these relationships.

Eternal submission has many areas of connection to theological anthropology because of the *imago Dei*. Bruce Ware is right to conclude, "We should therefore look more closely at just how the Son submits to his Father, and from this we may comprehend better how human relationships may best be understood and lived."[15]

---

13. The Hebrew construction of the phrase "one flesh" in Gen 2:24 is the same as in Deut 6:4 where God is spoken of as "one Lord." The "one flesh" in Gen 2:24 is not an absolute one (there are two persons involved), but a compound one. By means of comparison, the Hebrew text leaves room in Deut 6:4 for God as one in nature and yet eternally three persons.

14. See Melick, Jr. *Philippians, Colossians*, 307–20; Schreiner, *1, 2 Peter*, 125–68; Thielman, *Ephesians*, 365–411.

15. Ware, *Father, Son*, 73.

At the same time, we should be careful not to make unguarded inferences that might empower narcissistic, totalitarian individuals to force submission on others, or that might lay a burden of guilt on submissive parties so that they allow themselves to be shamed into obedience even when the authoritarian party might be abusing their authority to the harm of the one who submits. There is a careful, narrow path along which this doctrine should operate to allow redeemed individuals to image the triune God in terms of authority and submission.

Concluding Thoughts

Despite what some might believe, the battle for the doctrine of the eternal voluntary submission of the Son to the Father is not over. There are too many biblical texts and too much theological evidence that supports an internal order in the Trinity to just let the issue slide and fall into the messy abyss of mutually equal relations among the Trinitarian persons. This is not how the word of God presents their eternal relations and it is not how the church throughout history has viewed their relationships. The submission and obedience evident between Son and Father (and by extension, Spirit to Son and Father) during Jesus' earthly life has its ultimate corollary in the immanent, unending, eternal life of God.

Bibliography

Allen, David L. *Hebrews: An Exegetical and Theological Exposition of Holy Scripture.* Nashville: B&H Academic, 2010.

Ambrosiaster. *Commentaries on Romans and 1–2 Corinthians.* Ancient Christian Texts. Edited and translated by Gerald L. Bray. Downers Grove, IL: IVP Academic, 2009.

Angelici, Ruben. *Richard of Saint Victor, On the Trinity: English Translation and Commentary.* Eugene, OR: Cascade Books, 2011.

Aquinas, Thomas. *The "Summa Theologica" of St. Thomas Aquinas.* Literally translated by Fathers of the English Dominican Province. Reprinted ed. Westminster, MD: Christian Classics, 1981.

Barth, Karl. *Church Dogmatics.* Volume IV, Part 1. Edinburgh: T. & T. Clark, 1961.

Bartholomew, Craig G., and Heath A. Thomas, eds. *A Manifesto for Theological Interpretation.* Grand Rapids: Baker Academic, 2016.

Beale, G. K. "The Influence of Daniel upon the Structure and Theology of John's Apocalypse." *Journal of the Evangelical Theological Society* 27 (1984) 413–23.

Beeley, Christopher A. *The Unity of Christ: Continuity and Conflict in Patristic Tradition.* New Haven, CT: Yale University Press, 2012.

Berkhof, Louis. *Systematic Theology.* Grand Rapids: Eerdmans, 1996.

Bilezikian, Gilbert. "Hermeneutical Bungee-Jumping: Subordination in the Trinity." *Journal of the Evangelical Theological Society* 40 (1997) 57–68.

Billings, J. Todd. *The Word of God for the People of God: An Entryway to the Theological Interpretation of Scripture.* Grand Rapids: Eerdmans, 2010.

Branaman, Barry L. "The Egalitarian Use of the Trinity as a Model for Gender Relations." ThM thesis, Western Seminary, 2009.

Bray, Gerald, ed. *1–2 Corinthians.* Ancient Christian Commentary on Scripture. Downers Grove, IL: InterVarsity, 1999.

Butner, Jr., D. Glenn. "Eternal Functional Subordination and the Problem of the Divine Will." *Journal of the Evangelical Theological Society* 58 (2015) 131–49.

Bibliography

———. *The Son Who Learned Obedience: A Theological Case Against the Eternal Submission of the Son*. Eugene, OR: Pickwick, 2018.

Calvin, John. *The First Epistle of Paul the Apostle to the Corinthians*. Translated by John W. Fraser. Grand Rapids: Eerdmans, 1976.

Carson, D. A. "John 5:26: *Crux Interpretum* for Eternal Generation." In *Retrieving Eternal Generation,* edited by Fred Sanders and Scott R. Swain, 79–97. Grand Rapids: Zondervan, 2017.

Ciampa, Roy E., and Brian S. Rosner. *The First Letter to the Corinthians*. Grand Rapids: Eerdmans, 2010.

Claunch, Kyle. "God Is the Head of Christ: Does 1 Corinthians 11:3 Ground Gender Complementarity in the Immanent Trinity?" In *One God in Three Persons: Unity of Essence, Distinction of Persons, Implications for Life*, edited by Bruce A. Ware and John Starke, 65–93. Wheaton, IL: Crossway, 2015.

Cohick, Lynn H. *Philippians*. Edited by Tremper Longman III and Scot McKnight. Grand Rapids: Zondervan, 2013.

Cowen, Christopher W. "The Father and Son in the Gospel of John." In *One God in Three Persons: Unity of Essence, Distinction of Persons, Implications for Life*, edited by Bruce A. Ware and John Starke, 47–64. Wheaton, IL: Crossway, 2015.

Crisp, Oliver, and Fred Sanders, eds. *Advancing Trinitarian Theology: Explorations in Constructive Dogmatics*. Grand Rapids: Zondervan, 2014.

Crowe, Brandon D., and Carl R. Trueman, eds. *The Essential Trinity: New Testament Foundations and Practical Relevance*. Phillipsburg, NJ: P & R, 2017.

Cyril of Jerusalem. *Catechetical Letters*. A Select Library of Nicene and Post-Nicene Fathers of the Christian Church, 2.7:6–183. Edited by Philip Schaff and Henry Wace. Grand Rapids: Eerdmans, 1956.

De Smidt, Jacobus Christoffel. "A Meta-Theology of ὁ Θεός in Revelations 1:1–2." *Neotestamentica* 38 (2004) 183–208.

Edwards, Jonathan. *Notes on Scripture*. Edited by Stephen J. Stein. The Works of Jonathan Edwards, 15. New Haven, CT: Yale University Press, 1998.

Erickson, Millard. *Who's Tampering with the Trinity? An Assessment of the Subordination Debate*. Grand Rapids: Kregel Academic & Professional, 2009.

———. *God the Father Almighty: A Contemporary Exploration of the Divine Attributes*. Grand Rapids: Baker Books, 1998.

Fee, Gordon D. *Philippians*. The IVP New Testament Commentary Series 11. Downers Grove, IL: InterVarsity, 1999.

Giles, Kevin. "Defining the Error Called Subordinationism." *Evangelical Quarterly* 87 (2015) 207–24.

———. *Jesus and the Father: Modern Evangelicals Reinvent the Doctrine of the Trinity*. Grand Rapids: Zondervan, 2006.

———. "The Doctrine of the Trinity and Subordinationism." *Evangelical Review of Theology* 28 (2004) 270–84.

Bibliography

———. *The Eternal Generation of the Son: Maintaining Orthodoxy in Trinitarian Theology*. Downers Grove, IL: IVP Academic, 2012.

———. "The Evangelical Theological Society and the Doctrine of the Trinity." *The Evangelical Quarterly* 80 (2008) 323–38.

———. *The Rise and Fall of the Complementarian Doctrine of the Trinity*. Eugene, OR: Cascade Books, 2017.

———. "The Son of God Is Not Eternally Inferior, Subordinate, or Submissive." *Christian Research Journal* 31 (2008) 15–19.

———. *The Trinity & Subordinationism: The Doctrine of God & the Contemporary Gender Debate*. Downers Grove, IL: IVP Academic, 2002.

Goligher, Liam. "A Letter to Professors Grudem and Ware." *Housewife Theologian* (blog), *Mortification of Spin*, June 20, 2016, http://www.mortificationofspin.org/mos/housewife-theologian/a-letter-to-professors-grudem-and-ware.

———. "Dr. Liam Goligher Responds to Dr. Mike Ovey." *Housewife Theologian* (blog), *Mortification of Spin*, June 14, 2016, http://www.mortificationofspin.org/mos/housewife-theologian/dr-liam-goligher-responds-to-dr-mike-ovey.

———. "Is it Okay to Teach a Complementarianism Based on Eternal Subordination?" *Housewife Theologian* (blog), *Mortification of Spin*, June 3, 2016, http://www.alliancenet.org/mos/housewife-theologian/is-it-okay-to-teach-a-complementarianism-based-on-eternal-subordination#.XHisEPZFzIU.

———. "Reinventing God." *Housewife Theologian*. June 6, 2016. Accessed September 11, 2017, http://www.alliancenet.org/mos/housewife-theologian/reinventing-god#.XHisW_ZFzIU.

Grudem, Wayne. "Another Thirteen Evangelical Theologians Who Affirm the Eternal Submission of the Son to the Father." *Blog* (blog), *Reformation 21*, June 20, 2016, http://www.reformation21.org/blog/2016/06/another-thirteen-evangelical-t.php.

———. "Biblical Evidence for the Eternal Submission of the Son." In *The New Evangelical Subordinationism? Perspectives on the Equality of God the Father and God the Son*, edited by Dennis W. Jowers and H. Wayne House, 223–61. Eugene, OR: Wipf & Stock, 2012.

———. *Biblical Foundations for Manhood and Womanhood*. Wheaton, IL: Crossway, 2002.

———. "Doctrinal Deviations in Evangelical-Feminist Arguments about the Trinity." In *One God in Three Persons: Unity of Essence, Distinction of Persons, Implications for Life*, edited by Bruce A. Ware and John Starke, 17–45. Wheaton: Crossway, 2015.

———. *Systematic Theology: An Introduction to Biblical Doctrine*. Updated edition. Grand Rapids: Zondervan, 2000.

Hanson, Richard P. C. *The Search for the Christian Doctrine of God: The Arian Controversy 318–381*. Edinburgh: T. & T. Clark, 1988.

Hilary of Poitiers. *De Synodis*. A Select Library of Nicene and Post-Nicene Fathers of the Christian Church, 2.9a:4–29. Edited by Philip Schaff and Henry Wace. Grand Rapids: Eerdmans, 1956.

Bibliography

Hoekema, Anthony A. *Created in God's Image*. Grand Rapids: Eerdmans, 1994.

Holmes, Stephen R. "Trinitarian Action and Inseparable Operations: Some Historical and Dogmatic Reflections." In *Advancing Trinitarian Theology: Explorations in Constructive Dogmatics*, edited by Oliver Crisp and Fred Sanders, 60–74. Grand Rapids: Zondervan, 2014.

House, H. Wayne. "The Eternal Relational Subordination of the Son to the Father in Patristic Thought." In *The New Evangelical Subordinationism? Perspectives on the Equality of God the Father and God the Son*, edited by Dennis W. Jowers and H. Wayne House, 133–81. Eugene, OR: Wipf & Stock, 2012.

Irons, Charles Lee. "Let's Go Back to 'Only Begotten.'" *Charles Lee Irons* (blog), The Gospel Coalition, November 23, 2016, https://www.thegospelcoalition.org/article/lets-go-back-to-only-begotten.

———. "Μονογενής in the Church Fathers: A Response to Kevin Giles, Part 1." *Blog* (blog), The Upper Register, December 30, 2016, http://upper-register.typepad.com/blog/2016/12/%CE%BC%CE%BF%CE%BD%CE%CE%B3%CE%B5%CE%BD%CE%AE%CF%82-in-the-church-fathers-a-response-to-kevin-giles-part-1.html

Jeffery, Jack. "The 2016 Trinity Debate: A Bibliography." *THIRTY-SECOND UPDATED EDITION OF THE TRINITY DEBATE BIBLIOGRAPHY* (blog), Books at a Glance, November 9, 2017, http://www.booksataglance.com/blog/thirty-second-updated-edition-trinity-debate-bibliography.

Johnson, Keith E. "Trinitarian Agency and the Eternal Subordination of the Son: An Augustinian Perspective." *Themelios* 36 (2011) 7–25.

Jowers, Dennis W., and H. Wayne House, eds. *The New Evangelical Subordinationism? Perspectives on the Equality of God the Father and God the Son*. Eugene, OR: Wipf & Stock, 2012.

Kitano, Kenji. "The Eternal Relational Subordination of the Son to the Father." ThM thesis, Trinity Evangelical Divinity School, 1999.

Schrenk, Gottlob. "Βούλομαι, βουλη, βούλημα." In *Theological Dictionary of the New Testament*, edited by Gerhard Kittel and Gerhard Friedrich, 1:629-637. Grand Rapids: Eerdmans, 1984.

Köstenberger, Andreas J. *John*. 2nd edition. Grand Rapids: Baker Academic, 2004.

———. "Letter from Dr. Köstenberger." https://www.biblicalfoundations.org/letter-dr-kostenberger.

Kostenberger, Andreas J., and Scott R. Swain. *Father, Son and Spirit: The Trinity and John's Gospel*. Downers Grove, IL: IVP Academic, 2008.

Kovach, Stephen D. and Peter R. Schemm. "A Defense of the Doctrine of the Eternal Subordination of the Son." *Journal of the Evangelical Theological Society* 42 (1999) 464.

Leith, John H., ed. *Creeds of the Churches: A Reader in Christian Doctrine from the Bible to the Present*. 3rd edition. Atlanta: John Knox, 1982.

Letham, Robert. "Does the Son Submit to the Father in the Indivisible Unity of the Trinity?" *Christian Research Journal* 31 (2008) 12–15.

Bibliography

———. "Eternal Generation in the Church Fathers." In *One God in Three Persons: Unity of Essence, Distinction of Persons, Implications for Life*. Edited by Bruce A. Ware and John Starke, 109–25. Wheaton, IL: Crossway, 2015.

———. "Reply to Kevin Giles." *The Evangelical Quarterly* 80 (2008) 339–45.

———. *The Holy Trinity: In Scripture, History, Theology, and Worship*. Phillipsburg, NJ: P & R, 2004.

———. "The trdinationism: The Doctrine of God and the Contemporary Gender Debate." *Westminster Theological Journal* 65 (2003) 383–87.

Luther, Martin. "Commentary on 1 Corinthians 15." In *Luther's Works, Vol. 28: Selected Pauline Epistles*. Translated by Martin H. Bertram and edited by Hilton C. Oswald, 57–213. Saint Louis, MO: Concordia Publishing House, 2007.

Melick, Jr. Richard R. *Philippians, Colossians, Philemon*. Nashville: B & H, 1991.

Miller, Rachel. "Does The Son Eternally Submit To The Authority Of The Father?" *Practical Theology* (blog), *A Daughter of the Reformation*, May 28, 2015, https://adaughterofthereformation.wordpress.com /2015/05/28/does-the-son-eternally-submit-to-the-authority-of-the-father.

Morgan, Christopher W., and Robert A. Peterson, eds. *The Deity of Christ*. Theology in Community Series. Wheaton, IL: Crossway, 2011.

Morris, Leon L. *1 Corinthians*. Downers Grove, IL: IVP Academic, 2008.

Need, Stephen W. *Truly Divine and Truly Human: The Story of Christ and the Seven Ecumenical Councils*. Peabody, MA: Hendrickson, 2008.

Oliphint, K. Scott. "Simplicity, Triunity, and the Incomprehensibility of God." In *One God in Three Persons: Unity of Essence, Distinction of Persons, Implications for Life*, edited by Bruce A. Ware and John Starke, 215–35. Wheaton, IL: Crossway, 2015.

Osborne, Grant R. *Revelation*. Grand Rapids: Baker Academic, 2002.

Ovey, Michael J. *Your Will Be Done: Exploring Eternal Subordination, Divine Monarchy and Divine Humility*. Oxford: Latimer Trust, 2016.

———. "True Sonship—Where Dignity and Submission Meet." In *One God in Three Persons: Unity of Essence, Distinction of Persons, Implications for Life*, edited by Bruce A. Ware and John Starke, 127–54. Wheaton, IL: Crossway, 2015.

Rahner, Karl. *The Trinity*. Translated by Joseph Daniel. New York: Seabury, 1974.

Sanders, Fred. *The Deep Things of God: How the Trinity Changes Everything*. 2nd edition. Wheaton, IL: Crossway, 2017.

———. *The Triune God*. Edited by Michael Allen and Scott R. Swain. Grand Rapids: Zondervan, 2016.

———. "Things Eternal: Sonship, Generation, Generatedness." *Essay / Theology* (blog), *The Scriptorium Daily*, May 8, 2015, http://scriptoriumdaily.com/things-eternal-sonship-generation-generatedness.

Bibliography

———. "18 Theses on the Father and the Son." *Essay / Theology* (blog), *The Scriptorium Daily*, June 13, 2016, http://scriptoriumdaily.com/18-theses-on-the-father-and-the-son.

———. *The Image of the Immanent Trinity: Rahner's Rule and the Theological Interpretation of Scripture*. New York: Lang, 2005.

Sanders, Fred, and Scott R. Swain, eds. *Retrieving Eternal Generation*. Grand Rapids: Zondervan, 2017.

Schreiner, Thomas R. *1, 2 Peter, Jude*. Nashville: B & H, 2003.

Stevenson, James, and W. H. C. Frend, eds. *Creeds, Councils, and Controversies: Documents Illustrating the History of the Church, AD 337–461*. 3rd edition. Grand Rapids: Baker Acadmic, 2012.

Swain, Scott R. "The Mystery of the Trinity." In *The Essential Trinity: New Testament Foundations and Practical Relevance*, edited by Brandon D. Crown and Carl R. Trueman, 213–21. Phillipsburg, NJ: P&R Publishing, 2016.

Thielman, Frank. *Ephesians*. Grand Rapids: Baker Academic, 2010.

Thompson, Mark D. "The Trinity and Revelation." In *The Essential Trinity: New Testament Foundations and Practical Relevance*, edited by Brandon D. Crowe and Carl R. Trueman, 241–63. Phillipsburg, NJ: P & R, 2017.

Trueman, Carl. "A Rejoinder to Wayne Grudem." *Postcards from Palookaville* (blog), *Mortification of Spin*, June 9, 2016, http://www.mortificationofspin.org/node/40085.

———. "A Reply to Dr. Mohler on Nicene Trinitarianism." *Postcards from Palookaville* (blog), *Mortification of Spin*, June 28, 2016, http://www.mortificationofspin.org/node/40188.

———. "A Surrejoinder to Bruce Ware." *Postcards From Palookaville* (blog), *Mortification of Spin*, June 9, 2016, http://www.mortificationofspin.org/node/40084.

———. "Fahrenheit 381." *Postcards From Palookaville* (blog), *Mortification of Spin*, June 7, 2016, http://www.alliancenet.org/mos/postcards-from-palookaville/fahrenheit-381.

———. "In the End, it All Comes Down to This." *Postcards From Palookaville* (blog), *Mortification of Spin*, September 9, 2016, http://www.alliancenet.org/mos/postcards-from-palookaville/in-the-end-it-all-comes-down-to-this?#.XDQdvvZFzIU

———. "Motivated by Feminism? A Response to a Recent Criticism." *Postcards From Palookaville* (blog), *Mortification of Spin*, June 14, 2016, http://www.mortificationofspin.org/mos/postcards-from-palookaville/motivated-by-feminism-a-response-to-a-recent-criticism.

———. "Once More Unto the Breach . . . And Then No More: A final reply to Dr. Grudem." *Postcards From Palookaville* (blog), *Mortification of Spin*, June 21, 2016, http://www.alliancenet.org/mos/postcards-from-palookaville/once-more-unto-the-breach-and-then-no-more-a-final-reply-to-dr-grude.

Bibliography

Wallace, Daniel B. *Greek Grammar Beyond the Basics: An Exegetical Syntax of the New Testament with Scripture, Subject, and Greek Word Indexes.* Grand Rapids: Zondervan, 1997.

Ware, Bruce A. "Equal in Essence, Distinct in Roles: Eternal Functional Authority and Submission among the Essentially Equal Divine Persons of the Godhead." In *The New Evangelical Subordinationism? Perspectives on the Equality of God the Father and God the Son,* edited by Dennis W. Jowers and H. Wayne House, 13–38. Eugene, OR: Wipf & Stock, 2012.

———. *Father, Son, and Holy Spirit: Relationships, Roles, and Relevance.* Wheaton, IL: Crossway, 2005.

———. "Knowing the Self-Revealed God Who Is Father, Son, and Holy Spirit—Guest Post By Bruce Ware." *Biblical Reasoning* (blog), *Secundum Scripturas,* July 4, 2016, https://secundumscripturas.com/2016/07/04/knowing-the-self-revealed-god-who-is-father-son-and-holy-spirit.

Ware, Bruce A. and John Starke. *One God in Three Persons: Unity of Essence, Distinction of Persons, Implications for Life.* Wheaton, IL: Crossway, 2015.

Index

Acts 13:30–37, on fulfillment of Old Testament promises, 92–93
Acts 27:12 and 27:42, use of "counsel" (βουλὴ) in, 99n62
Adam, links to Christ, 48, 50–52
Ambrosiaster, 65–66
Arianism
   and controversies associated with the Trinity, 64
   and criticisms of ESS as, 2
   Giles's views, 17–18
Athanasius, 18
Augustine of Hippo (St. Augustine)
   and Giles's views on the role of the Son in the Trinity, 19
   Johnson's views on, 65n6
   on separation of human and divine Christs, 64–65

Barth, Karl, 126
Basil, 67n12
begotten, as a term, 113–17. *See also* eternal generation; "only begotten" (μονογενὴς)
Bilezikian, Gilbert, 67n12
Butner, D. Glenn Jr., 50–51, 102–3
Byrd, Amiee, 2

Calvin, John, 72
Carson, D. A., 119, 119n121
chain of revelation, 53–55, 53n50
Christ (Χριστός). *See also* the Son (Jesus Christ)
   as a second Adam, 50–51
   as a term, Paul's use of, 59
Chrysostom, 65
church history
   authority of, True's view, 28
   and diverse views on ESS, 17–18, 63
   and Nicene Trinitarianism, x
   patristic views on submission, 67n12
   and theological interpretation of Scripture (TIS), 62–63
   for understanding eternal submission, 5–6, 62
   for understanding Scripture, x, 75
Clampa, Roy E., 58–59
Claunch, Kyle, 97–98
Cohick, Lynn, 44, 45n32, 47n37
complementarians
   criticisms of ESS, 28–29
   debates about eternal submission, 2
   views on the Trinity, 4, 4n10, 21–22

139

Index

1 Corinthians 11
   cautions about interpreting, 60
   context for, 58
   and the hierarchical structure of the Trinity, 59
   meaning of head (κεφαλή), debates about, 58
1 Corinthians 11:3
   as a difficult text, 127n9
   and Christ's post-resurrection submission to God, 4
   and gender relationships, 20, 56–57, 126–27
   and *taxis* within the Trinity, 9–10
1 Corinthians 15:20–28
   Ambrosaister's interpretation, 65–66
   Butner's interpretation, 50
   Calvin's interpretation, 72
   evidence for the ESS, 47–48, 51–52
   Giles's interpretations, 20, 49–50
   historical interpretations, 5
   Luther's commentary on, 73–74
   medieval interpretations, 68–71
   modern interpretations, 75–77
   Morris's interpretation, 49
   patristic interpretations, 63–67
   support for ESS, 5, 10, 47–49
   Theodoret of Cyr's interpretation, 64
Council of Chalcedon
   Definition of Chalcedon, 97–98
   definition of the relationship of the divine and human Christ, 92–93
Council of Ephesus, condemnation of Nestorius at, 92
"counsel" (βουλή), as a collective term, 99, 99nn60–63
Cowen, Christopher, 35n16
the creation, 108
Cyril of Alexandria, 91–92

Cyril of Jerusalem, 66–67

Daniel 2:28–29, 2:45, reference to in Revelation 1:1, 53–54
Definition of Chalcedon, 97–98
De Synodis (Hilary of Poitier), 68
divine simplicity, immutability
   and arguments against ESS, 6, 24–25, 27, 94–95
   and arguments supporting ESS, 96–98, 101–2
   incorporation of both unity and diversity, 82
   modalist views, 100, 100n63
divine will
   and arguments related to ESS, 6n11, 25, 79–83
   and divine freedom, 98–99
   and personal distinctions, 98–101
   and the Son's voluntary subordination, 102–5

Eastern theology, Trinitarian views, ix
ecclesio-historical baggage, 14n46
economic Trinity. *See* immanent and economic Trinity
Edwards, Jonathan, 74–75
EFS (eternal functional subordination), 3, 7–8
egalitarians. *See also* Giles, Kevin
   criticisms of ESS, 4, 16, 28–29
   defined, 1–2n1
   and gender reciprocity, 13
Ephesians 1:10, Paul's view of Christ in, 59
Ephesians 1:11, and multiple facets of the unified divine will, 98–99
Ephesians 1:20
   emphasis on the Father's authority, 85–86

Index

reading in conjunction with
John 17:5, 86n18
Ephesians 3:4, and the mystery of
Christ, 59–60
ERAS (eternal roles of authority and
submission), 3–4
Erickson, Millard
arguments against ESS, 79–86,
94–95, 114
on God's capacity for sin, 104
on the Son as necessarily
subordinate, 102
ESS. *See* eternal submission of the
Son (ESS)
eternal functional subordination
(EFS), 3, 7–8
eternal generation
Aquinas's teachings, 70
description and historical
understanding, 112–13
Ericson's and Ware's critiques of,
114–16
and eternal submission, 6,
120–21
evangelical support for, 116
and the Father-Son relationship,
3–4, 75–76, 83
Giles's views, 21
and human generation, 120
and the inseparable operations
of the Trinity, 111–12
Letham's views, 113–14
as relationship as opposed to
action, 118–19, 118n117
True's views, 27, 27n50
eternal submission of the Son (ESS).
See also God the Father;
Father-Son relationship *and
specific scriptural references*
and the absence of hierarchy
within the Trinity, 83
Ambrosaister's views, 65–66

arguments against, overview
and comparisons, 6, 28–29,
55–56, 55–56n57
avoiding authoritarian
interpretations of, 128–29
as biblically fallacious, 19
and the chain of revelation, 55
as consistent with simultaneous
full divinity, 79–86
core understanding, xii
Cyril of Jerusalem's views 15:28,
66–67
definition, 14–15
and divine freedom, 98–99,
102–5
and divine simplicity, 24–25,
94–98, 101–2
and divine unity, 79–86
and eternal generation, 83,
111–21
and the Father's authority, x, 33,
38–43, 50, 71, 85
and freedom of inclination, 103,
105
Giles's views, 1–2, 17–19, 49–50,
57–59, 115–16
Goligher's views, 2n7, 4, 21–23,
25–26, 81, 86–87, 106
Grudem's views, 3, 7–8, 10n31,
27, 27n50, 56, 58, 115–16
historical interpretations, 17,
68–74, 75–77
and human relationships, 125–
27, 129–30, 127n10
and the immanent and
economic Trinity, 21–22,
50, 86–91, 122–24, 126n7,
128n12
implications for theological
anthropology, 124–30
implications for Trinitarian
theology, xii, 1–3, 6, 21,
106–12, 122–24
Johnson's views, 65n6

141

Index

eternal submission of the Son (*continued*)
    Letham's views, 11–14. 11m32
    ongoing debates about, x, xii–xiii, 1–2, 62, 97
    supporting evidence from Scripture, 32–38, 40–62
    terms used to describe, 3–4, 4n9
    theological importance, xi
    Trueman's views, 2, 4, 4n10, 21, 26–28

the Father. *See* Father-Son relationship; God the Father
Father, Son, & Holy Spirit: Relationships, Roles, and Relevance (Ware), 9–10
Father-Son relationship. *See also* ESS (eternal submission of the Son); God the Father; the Son (Jesus Christ)
    as aspirational model, 126
    and the balance between essence and diversity, 121
    and eternal generation, 3–4, 75–76, 83
    and in the Gospel of John, 30–32
    as model for human relationships, 3, 126
    and mutual submission, 48n39
    patristic views, 64–67
    post-resurrection, 56
    and relational submission, 79–81, 81n6
    unity of, and debates about ESS, 90–93
freedom
    divine, and divine will, 98–99
    of inclination, 105
    libertarian, limits of, 104–5

    and voluntary submission, 12–14, 36–38, 43–46, 67. 104–5, 122, 126–30
"full account" (*exēgēsato*), 32–33
functional submission, 3, 7–8, 20, 52

gender relationships
    arguments related to ESS, 62
    and humans as *imago Dei*, 125–26, 125n5, 126n7
    Letham's views, 13
Gethsemane, Jesus's prayer in, 100–102
Giles, Kevin
    on beliefs of past theologians, 75
    on Christ's changing status following resurrection, 41n26
    critique of Grudem, 8
    on EFS and the Arian heresy, 17–18, 18n12
    on EFS and gender roles, 17
    and the egalitarian perspective, 4n10, 16
    emphasis on God's unity/oneness, 29, 80
    on equality in the Trinity, 19–20
    on eternal generation, 116, 117–20
    on eternal submission, 1–2
    on the immanent and economic Trinity, 89n24, 119–20
    on Jesus's God-like humanity, 38n21
    on relational subordination, 68, 71n24
    Letham's criticisms of, 12–13, 23n33
    on misuse of ESS, 18
    on mutual submission between Father and Son, 48n39
    on scholarly support for arguments, 18

Index

Scriptural support for arguments, 19, 49–50, 57–59, 115–16
on sending the coequal Son into the world, 34
on "voluntary subordination," 128n11
God the Father. *See also* Father-Son relationship; the Son (Jesus Christ)
ad intra vs. *ad extra* acts, 118
asymmetrical relationship with the Son, 119
authority of, x, 33, 38–43, 50, 71, 85
and the begetting of the Son, 40–41, 113
capacity for sin, 104
and the chain of revelation, 53–55
Christ's subjection to, 15:28, 49
direct rule of, 50
and the divine identity vs. divine diversity, 82
and divine obedience, 126
and the divine planning of Jesus' priesthood, 39–40
and divine simplicity, 24–25, 94–98, 101–2
and divine will, 25, 97–101, 109–10, 101n70, 120–21
essence and dignity of, 69
and eternal generation of the Son, 83
as eternally equal to the Son, 70
external vs. internal authority, 83–86, 86n17
freedom of, characteristics, 105
"full account" (*exēgēsato*) of through the Son, 31–33
as giver, 69–70, 70n18
and God's will, 12, 59, 97–100–102, 101n70

and humans as *imago Dei*, 125–26, 125n5, 126n7
internal relations and external functions, 124
necessary subordination of the Son to, 102
as ontologically unified with his Son, 74
as origin of Christ's revelation, 31–32, 52–53
self-revelation in Christ, Goligher's view, 25
as sender, not sent, 36
shared goal with the Son, 37n18
submission of the Son to, working definition, 14–15
as Supreme Orderer, 74–75
as unitary vs. triune, ix–xi, 22–23, 29, 94, 96, 125n6
"God Who Sends God" (Sanders), 88–89
Goligher, Liam
commitment to divine simplicity/unity, 95
criticisms of ESS, 2n7, 4, 21–23, 25–26, 81, 86–87, 106
critique of Grudem, 24
on eternal generation, 116
on the immanent Trinity, 22
on the limitations of the incarnate Christ, 26
on submission and redemption, 2
on the Trinity as model for human behavior, 124–25n4
Gregory of Nazianzus, 27, 94
Gregory of Nyssa, 67n12
Grudem, Wayne
accusation of heresy against, 3
criticisms of, 8, 17, 24
on divine simplicity, 95–96
on eternal generation, 27, 27n50
on eternal submission, 7–8

Index

Grudem, Wayne (*continued*)
   on the Father's sending the Son into the world, 34
   focus on roles/functions of the Trinity, 10
   influence and impact, 8
   scriptural support for arguments, 10n31, 56, 58, 115–16
   on the Son's submission as necessary, not voluntary, 103
   use of term "subordination," 8

head (κεφαλή), headship, 19, 56, 58
Hebrews 1:5, and the exaltation of the risen Christ, 41
Hebrews 4:14–5:10
   and Christ's preincarnate submission, 4
   and Christ's priesthood, 38–39, 39n24
   and the Father's authority over the Son, 43
   and Jesus's humanity and empathy, 39
   reference to Psalm 110:4, 42
heresy, and discussions of eternal submission, xi, 3, 13, 17–18, 27–28, 82, 93
Hilary of Poitiers, 68, 68–69n16
Hoekema, Anthony A., 125n6
Holmes, Stephen, 106–7, 111n95
Holy Spirit
   and the chain of revelation, 33, 53n50
   as fully God, 14, 36, 98, 107, 122
   obedience of, 7
   origins of, 23, 23n33
   and theological interpretation of Scripture, 62–63
   and Trinitarian relations, 126
The Holy Trinity (Letham), ix
Horrell, J. Scott, 102–3

Houghton, Myron, ix
House, H. Wayne, 75–76
human beings, 110–12. *See also* hypostatic union
   authority given to by God, 125–26
   as complementary with the divine, 12
   and gender relationships, 126–27, 129
   and *imago Dei*, 125–26, 125n5
   and the model of divine obedience, 126
   natural order among, as reflection of divine *taxis*, 10
hypostatic union, doctrine of
   and the chain of revelation, 55
   and Christ's eternal humanity, 51, 73–74
   and ESS, 12

imago Dei, 125–26, 125n5, 126n7
immanent and economic Trinity
   Giles's views, 89n27, 119–20
   and inseparable operations, 110
   interrelationship between, 21–22, 50, 86–91, 122–24, 126n7, 128n12
   Sanders's definition, 88
   and the unity of God's will, 97
inclination, freedom of, 105
inseparable operations of Trinitarian persons
   as applying exclusively to God's economic life, 110–11
   as argument against ESS, 6, 106
   conflicting scholarly views on, 107
   the creation as an example of, 108
   and eternal generation, arguments associated with, 111–12

Index

Ware's view, 107–8
Irons, Lee, 116–17

Jesus (Ἰησοῦς). *See also* the Son
    (Jesus Christ)
  authority over followers, 35–36
  prayer in the Garden of
    Gethsemane, 100
  Paul's use of, 59
Jesus and the Father (Giles), ix
John, Gospel of
  and the chain of revelation,
    53–55
  emphasis on the closeness of
    Father-Son relationship, 32
  and God as spirit, 31
  and Jesus's voluntarily
    submission, 38
  "sending" terminology in, 34–35
  Shaliach, Giles's interpretation,
    20
  the Son as united with yet
    distinct from the Father,
    30–31
  John 1:1-4, and Jesus as both equal
    and relational with God,
    30–31
  John 1:18, and Jesus as both equal
    and relational with God,
    31, 91
  John 1:22, "sending" terminology
    used in, 35
  John 1:24, "sending" terminology
    used in, 34–35
  John 1:33, distinguishing between
    the sender and the sent in,
    35
  John 5:17–18, and the unity of the
    Son's work with that of the
    Father, 109
  John 5:26, on the Father-Son
    relationship, 119n121
  John 6:38-40
    and Christ's preincarnate
      submission, 4
    and the obedience inherent in
      the Father-Son relationship,
      33n12, 37–38
  John 8, Ware's interpretation, 9–10
  John 13:16, and the subordination
    of the messenger, 34–35
  John 13:20, and Jesus's sending of
    his followers into the world,
    35
  John 14:25, and the sending of the
    Holy Spirit by the Father and
    the Son, 36
  John 14:28, Giles's interpretation, 19
  John 15:26, and the sending of the
    Holy Spirit by the Father and
    the Son, 36
  John 16:7, and the sending of the
    Holy Spirit by the Father and
    the Son, 36
  John 17:5, and Jesus's status
    following his exultation,
    42n28
  John 20:21, and Jesus's sending of
    his followers into the world,
    35–36
  John 39, and the obedience
    intrinsic to the Father-Son
    relationship, 37
Johnson, Keith E., 65n6, 77
John the Baptist, 35, 35n16

Knight, George W. III, 17
Köstenberger, Andreas J., 31–33

Letham, Robert
  on Augustine's views of the
    Trinity, 71n22
  on Calvin's views on 1
    Corinthians 15:27–28, 72

Index

Letham, Robert (*continued*)
  commentary on 1 Corinthians 11:3, 57
  conversations with Giles, x, 43–44
  critique of Bilezikian, 67n12
  on Jesus's submissive altruism/submission, 49, 45–46
  on Jesus's voluntary self-emptying, 43–44
  position on ESS, 11–14, 11n32
  on the revelatory purpose of Jesus's incarnation, 11
  on submission and divine freedom, 103
  on "subordination" as a term, 13
  on the *taxis* among Trinitarian persons, 118–19
Levitical priests, call to service by God, 39
libertarian freedom, limits of, 104–5
Lister, J. Ruan, ix
Luther, Martin, 73–74

male headship, 19, 56
Matthew 11:25–27, twofold description of the Trinity in, 82
Matthew 22:41–46, reference to Psalm 110:1 in, 50n43
Matthew 28:18
  and Giles's rejection of arguments about ESS, 18–19
  and external and internal divine authority, 85, 85–86n16
Melick, Richard Jr., 45, 84n15, 85n15
Miller, Rachel, 2
Moody, Dale, 115
Morris, Leon, 49

Nestorianism
  and differences between the incarnate and the divine Christ, 91–93
  Calvin's similarities with, 74
  defined, 55–56n57
  and hypostatic union, 55–56
Nicene Creed, Nicene Trinitarianism
  authority of, x
  and divine simplicity, 27, 94–95
  and equality within the Trinity, 83
  and ESS, 2, 26–28
  and eternal generation, 120
  Goligher's views on, 23

obedience to God. See ESS (eternal submission of the son)
Oecumenius, 70–71, 70n20, 71n23
Old Testament
  father-son relationships, 33
  foretelling of Christ in, 40–43
Oliphint, K. Scott, 96–97
"only begotten" (μονογενὴς). See also eternal generation
  Aquinas's views, 70
  and Christ's humanity and divinity, 92
  debates about meaning of, 115, 116–17
  and paternal authority, 68–69n16
  and voluntary obedience, 67
ontological submission, 20, 82
Ovey, Michael J., 76–77, 100–102, 101n70

Paul. *See also specific scriptural references*
  on the authority of the Father, 85–86, 86n17

Index

on the Father-Son relationship
  after the resurrection, 48–50
  on Jesus's submission, 44, 47
  on Jesus's seat on the right hand
    of God, 85–86
  use of terms "Christ" (Χριστός)
    and "Jesus" (Ἰησοῦς), 59
1 Peter 2:18–25, support for eternal
    submission in, 10, 128
Philippians 2:1–4, emphasis on
    altruism and humility, 44
Philippians 2:5–11
  on Christ's ministry and post-
    resurrection submission to
    God, 4, 47
  and distinctions inherent in
    divine will, 99–100
  and the Father's authority over
    the Son, 43–47
  Giles's exegesis of, 19
  and the interplay between
    external and internal divine
    authority, 84
priesthood, Jesus's
  evidence from Psalm 2:7, 40–42
  evidence from Psalm 110:4,
    42–43
  God as source of, 39–40, 40n25
  high priest qualifications, 39
  as permanent, 42
Psalm 2:7, referencing in the New
  Testament, 40–41
Psalm 8:6, references to the New
  Testament, 50
Psalm 110:1
  reference to in 1 Corinthians 15,
    48, 50
  reference to in Matthew 22:41–
    46, 50n43
Psalm 110:4
  application to Christ, 40
  as support for ESS, 42–43
  "putting under" terminology, Paul's
    use of, 49–50

Rahner, Karl (Rahner's Rule)
  on the immanent and economic
    Trinity, 6, 89, 89n24
  influence, 87
  on submission, 18
redemption, covenant of, 25
Reformation period, assessments of
    ESS during, 72–74
regard (ἡγήσατο), as concept in
    Philippians, 43, 45–46
relationality. *See* Father-Son
    relationship
resurrection, Jesus's
  and the exaltation of the Son, 17,
    40–43, 41n26, 41n27, 42n28,
    59, 69n16, 85–86, 86n18
  and the immanent relationship
    of Son and the Father, 42n28
  and Jesus's obedience to the
    Father's authority, 36–38, 60
  order of events associated with,
    48
  as realization of Old Testament
    promises, 40–42
Retrieving Eternal Generation
  (Sanders and Swain, eds.),
    117
Revelation, book of
  as both the word of God and the
    witness to the word, 54n55
  and the chain of revelation,
    53–55, 53n50
  on Christ's post-resurrection
    submission to God, 5
  opening phrases, 52–53
  support for ESS in, 52–56
Richard of Saint Victor, 70
Romans 5:12–21, and Adam's
    authority over Eve, 13
Rosner, Brian S., 58–59

147

Index

Sanders, Fred
  on eternal generation, 116
  on the Father-Son relationship, 90–91
  on God's internal and external works, 110n92, 118n118
  on the immanent and economic Trinity, 87–89
  on interpreting 1 Corinthians 11:3, 58
  on the Trinity as model for human behavior, 124–25n4
Schrenk, Gottlob, 99n61
Scripture. *See also specific scriptural references*
  as basis for understanding xii, ESS, 3–5, 61, 10n31
  as both of God and about God, 53n49
  citing the church fathers on, caution, 77–78
  and support for a faceted divine will, 82, 84–85, 98–100
  as ultimate authority, x–xi, 23, 28, 50
self-emptying, the Son's, 12, 44–46
"send" (πεμπω), sending terminology, 33–36
Shaliach concept, 20, 34–35
"show" (δεῖξαι), as term in Revelation, 53
simplicity, divine. *See also* Nicene Creed
  and arguments against ESS, 6, 24–25, 29, 94–95, 107
  and arguments supporting ESS, 96–99, 101, 123
sin, God's capacity for, 104
the Son (Jesus Christ). *See also* Christ (Χριστός); ESS (eternal submission of the Son); Father-Son relationship; God the Father
  appointment as high priest, 42–43
  asymmetrical relationship with the Father, 119, 122
  authority, 34–35, 85, 85–86n16
  as begotten by the Father, 41, 68–69n16, 70, 70n18, 84, 113
  as both human and divine, 7–8, 50n43, 51, 64, 73, 91–93
  as equal and identical to the Father, 19, 70, 113
  essence and dignity of, 69
  and eternal generation, 21, 27, 83
  as eternally submissive, 3, 48–49, 48n38, 74, 82–86
  exaltation following resurrection, 17, 40–43, 41n26, 41n27, 42n28, 59, 69n16, 85–86, 86n18
  and hypostatic union, 51
  incarnation of, revelatory role, 10–11, 31–32, 33n12, 35, 51, 53–55
  names used for, 59–60
  as receiver, Aquinas's view, 69–70, 70n18
  role within the Trinity, 19
  shared goal with the Father, 37n18
  submission/subordination/obedience to the Father, 14–15, 30–31, 33, 60, 71, 102
  voluntary nature of submission, 12–14, 36–38, 43–46, 67, 104–5, 122, 126–30
"Son," as a term in Scripture, 3
submission. *See also* ESS (eternal submission of the Son); Father-Son relationship; God the Father; the Son
  Aquinas's teachings, 68

Index

and the distinction between
function and roles, 7–8
and freedom, 102–5
in human relations, 126–27,
127n10, 129–30
subordination vs., 11, 13–14, 70
Swain, Scott, 33, 82
Systematic Theology (Grudem),
7–8, 17

taxis (order), 9, 118–19
Theodoret of Cyr, 64
theological anthropology,
implications of ESS for, 33,
70n18, 124–30
theological interpretation of
Scripture (TIS), 62–63
Thomas Aquinas
ad intra vs. *ad extra* acts, 118
on 1 Corinthians 15:28, 68
on natural order in the Trinity,
68
recognition of God's "paternal
authority," 68–69
views on eternal submission,
69–70, 70n18
1 Timothy 2:8–15, and the ordering
of human relationships,
127n9
Trinitarian debate of 2016, x, 4n10,
107
Trinitarian theology.
the Trinity. *See also* ESS (eternal
submission of the Son);
God the Father; the Son;
submission
and the Arian controversy, 64
and the economy of salvation,
19, 89n24
immanent and economic
aspects, 6, 122–24

and inseparable operations
of Trinitarian persons, 6,
106–12
intra-Trinitarian relationships,
101–2
the knowable and the
unknowable, 43
spiration as factor
differentiating, 23–24
Trinitarian relations and roles,
1–3, 5–8, 98, 126
taxis of authority and
submission, 9–10
and the unitary vs. triune God,
ix–xi, 22–23, 29, 94, 96,
125n63
The Trinity & Subordinationism
(Giles), 18
Trinity debate of 2016, x, xii–xiii,
1–2, 62, 97
tritheism, 2, 94, 95, 107
The Triune God (Sanders), 88–89
Trueman, Carl
arguments against ESS, 2, 4,
4n10, 21, 26–28
commitment to divine
simplicity/unity, 94
on eternal generation, 116
on the nature of God's will, 97

Urlsperger, Johann August, 88–89

Wallace, Daniel B., 46n36
Ware, Bruce
accusation of heresy against, 3
on the authority of the Father,
56, 58
discussion of *taxis*, 9–10
on eternal generation, 27,
27n50, 114
on the Father-Son relationship,
56, 130

Index

Ware, Bruce (*continued*)
    focus on the eternal when citing Scripture, 10n31
    on inseparable operations, 107–8
    on the limits of libertarian freedom, 104–5
    on meaning of head (κεφαλὴ) in 1 Corinthians 11:3, 58
will, God's. *See* God the Father

women
    and husband-wife relationships, 126–27, 129
    role in church, and debates about eternal submission, 1–2n1, 17, 24–25
    submission by, 18–19, 56–60

www.ingramcontent.com/pod-product-compliance
Lightning Source LLC
Chambersburg PA
CBHW051104160426
43193CB00010B/1312